RELILIV
6.99

D0801510

IN PRAISE OF

plan b

IN PRAISE OF

plan b

MOVING FROM
"WHAT IS" TO "WHAT CAN BE"

DR. TIM KIMMEL

ZONDERVAN®   A WORTHY BOOK

ZONDERVAN.com/
AUTHORTRACKER
follow your favorite authors

ZONDERVAN

In Praise of Plan B
Copyright © 2010 by Tim Kimmel

This title is also available as a Zondervan ebook. Visit www.zondervan.com/ebooks.

This title is also available in a Zondervan audio edition. Visit www.zondervan.fm.

Requests for information should be addressed to:

Zondervan, *Grand Rapids, Michigan 49530*

Library of Congress Cataloging-in-Publication

Kimmel, Tim.
   In praise of plan B : moving from "what is" to "what can be" / Tim Kimmel.
      p. cm.
   Includes bibliographical references.
   ISBN 978-0-310-32752-3 (hardcover, jacketed)
   1. Christian life. 2. Christian life—Anecdotes. I. Title.
BV4501.3.K5525   2010
248.4—dc22   2010029171

All Scripture quotations, unless otherwise indicated, are taken from the Holy Bible, *New International Version®, NIV®.* Copyright © 1973, 1978, 1984 by Biblica, Inc.™ Used by permission of Zondervan. All rights reserved worldwide.

All Scripture references marked NASB are taken from the *New American Standard Bible®.* Copyright © 1960, 1962, 1968, 1971, 1972, 1973, 1975, 1977, 1995 by The Lockman Foundation. Used by permission.

Any Internet addresses (websites, blogs, etc.) and telephone numbers printed in this book are offered as a resource. They are not intended in any way to be or to imply an endorsement by Zondervan, nor does Zondervan vouch for the content of these sites and numbers for the life of this book.

All rights reserved. No part of this publication may be reproduced, stored in a retrieval system, or transmitted in any form or by any means—electronic, mechanical, photocopy, recording, or any other—except for brief quotations in printed reviews, without the prior permission of the publisher.

Some of the names and details in this book have been changed to protect people's privacy.

Packaged by Worthy Media. For subsidiary and foreign language rights, contact info@worthymedia.com.

Cover design: Faceout Studio, Jason Gabbert
Interior design: Inside Out Design and Typesetting

Printed in the United States of America

10 11 12 13 14 15 /RRD/ 25 24 23 22 21 20 19 18 17 16 15 14 13 12 11 10 9 8 7 6 5 4 3 2 1

OTHER BOOKS BY TIM KIMMEL

Little House on the Freeway
Raising Kids Who Turn Out Right
Homegrown Heroes
The High Cost of High Control
Basic Training for a Few Good Men
Grace Based Parenting
Why Christian Kids Rebel
50 Ways to Really Love Your Kids
Raising Kids for True Greatness
Extreme Grandparenting: The Ride of Your Life

For more helpful family resources by
Dr. Kimmel, go to:
www.familymatters.net

To Mike, Lauren, and Ian

You were grafted in through your marriage
to our kids and have each brought
so much goodness to our family tree.

CONTENTS

CONTENTS

ACKNOWLEDGMENTS

Publishing is more rewarding when you've got friends like Steve Green and Byron Williamson believing in you; compelling ideas are more forthcoming when you have a woman like Darcy whispering in your ear; huge challenges are easier to overcome when you have people like the great team at Family Matters cheering you on; and finishing a manuscript makes an author a better man when you have champions like Tom Williams, Rob Birkhead, and Jennifer Stair making sure they've drawn out your best.

For all the above, I am grateful. Without them, this book wouldn't exist.

INTRODUCTION:
IN PRAISE OF PLAN B

When I sat down so long ago to write down my goals and set my path for the future, I didn't plan on the rocks that would block my way or the scars that would crisscross my will. Back then I believed that plans had power and that success was just skill and talent harnessed to the right opportunity.

But somewhere along my drive through the dreams I paved in my mind, I hit some potholes. And then life laid out some speed bumps that wrecked my alignment and broke my concentration. It was hard to learn such a big lesson so early, yet it was probably for the best.

Reality pulled my ear up close to her lips and whispered the truth: "Life's not fair, boy. Accept it. You'll last longer."

I denied that truth for a while and then fought it for a long time. But little by little, that truth began to wash away the illusion I had embraced as a young man, and it seeped through a few weak seams in my soul. It's not fair, for instance, that . . .

. . . you study harder, make better grades, get up earlier, and stay at work later, but they pick the other guy anyway.

. . . your hair turns gray, your gums recede, and you wake up one morning to find long hairs growing from your ears.

. . . you resign yourself to a budget, buy groceries with coupons, and save up all year for enough to get the whole family into Disneyland for a day, and when you get there and buy your tickets, you find out that the Indiana Jones Adventure ride is closed for repairs.

. . . no matter how many miles you run at dawn or how many bowls of oatmeal you scarf down before you leave for work, your pants get tighter every year.

. . . you wait for years to get your name in the paper, and when you finally do, they spell it wrong.

. . . you finally get your kids in an ideal school district and an exciting youth group, and then your boss transfers you and your family to another time zone.

. . . the phone doesn't ring with the news of the full scholarship.

. . . the mail doesn't carry the hoped-for financial relief from some unknown relative who died and left it all to you.

So here I sit, neither by default nor in defeat, the patron saint of Plan B.

I pour another five hundred bucks into a ten-year-old car to avoid a car payment. I sit on the carpet next to the piano bench and listen to a ten-year-old play her recital piece for the thirtieth time. I cut my own grass, wash my own car, and shine my own shoes. I travel coach and get excited when I see a Denny's restaurant sign in the distance. I stay up late at my computer, trying to stretch a paycheck past another orthodontist bill. And I sleep in mismatched pajamas with my arm over the waist of a wife who cries over the Flintstones version of *A Christmas Carol.*

Most of us didn't get Plan A. Some still believe it will happen, though—they can't believe it would be denied. Others have long since turned bitter and indifferent because Plan B wasn't supposed to happen to them.

But as a card-carrying member of the Plan B Club, I've learned a few things about it along the way. Average is not that bad. Obscurity plays well after you get used to it. Pride is tough to swallow, but it doesn't leave a bitter aftertaste. And Plan A . . . well, it is highly overrated. So are success, wealth, and fame.

Plan A has a bad habit of defining you, whereas Plan B seems to fit like a well-worn pair of old work boots. And it keeps the things that could distract us from blocking the things that matter most. Plan B allows us enough time to taste the coffee, smell the lilacs, and pick up the rhythm. It keeps us from believing in ourselves so much that we forget to trust God. It helps us identify with a blue-collar Savior who died on a cross to give all the people on Plan B a reason to hold their heads high.

This book is about those people. The stories you'll

read here are a selection from blogs and essays I've written over the years about people who had less than they wanted, who faced things they'd rather have avoided, and who made tough decisions that turned them off the Plan A freeway onto the potholed asphalt of a Plan B back road.

Only one or two of these people did something that put their names in the history books. Most lived in unnoticed corners, remaining unknown and unsung. Average people doing average things. Some faced life-and-death challenges, some gave up big dreams to do the right thing, while others merely coped with the inconvenience of the moment.

But what we sometimes fail to realize is that real heroism is not merely working up the courage to kill a giant. It's more commonly sticking to the mundane duty in front of you, day in and day out. Dealing with everyday breakdowns and annoyances with grace. Keeping on keeping on. As British explorer Henry Stanley told reporters of his successful African expedition to find David Livingstone, "It wasn't the lions and tigers that bothered us; it was the gnats."

Whether fighting lions and tigers or gnats, the people I've written of here were infused with an extra helping of God's grace that enabled them to make their Plan B lives shine with the glow of heaven's light.

So with this book I lift my glass of Alka-Seltzer and toast all who take rank in the army of the average, the mundane, and the predictable. "To Plan B—not the best, but clearly the better. Cheers!"

PART 1
*Facing Black-and-White Reality
with Technicolor Dreams*

1

LOST IN BEDFORD FALLS

There's a little town I want you to visit. You've been there several times already—at least most of you have. We go there every Christmas, as most others do, but it's a good place to visit any time, any season. Some of you haven't had the chance to go there yet, but you need to take the next opportunity you get. Just hit the turn signal, veer down the off-ramp, and follow the signs to Bedford Falls. It's an interesting mix of nobodies and everybodies smack-dab in the heartland of us all. Trust me, if you haven't seen Frank Capra's movie *It's a Wonderful Life,* you must make the trip. And the sooner, the better.

We own three copies of the movie. Two are the original black-and-white production. The third is a colorized version. All tell the same story of a small-town boy who dreams of traveling the main streets of the world, building bridges that span the widest rivers and skyscrapers that rub shoulders with the clouds. There's only one problem: this boy grows up to be a man of character, courage, and commitment.

Meet George Bailey. When his father died, the struggling family business—Bailey Building and Loan—finds itself at the mercy of the heartless Mr. Potter. He's the evil and greedy antagonist who wants to own the town and everyone in it. The only one who can stand up to Mr. Potter is the young George Bailey. Without George, Bedford Falls would slide into moral ruin and financial slavery.

So young George assumes the helm of his father's dream long enough to become trapped by a series of circumstances too hard to avoid. He marries Mary, the girl who's had a crush on him since her early rendezvous at Gower's Pharmacy. They have four kids and do their best to raise them in the drafty old mansion. Meanwhile, everyone's ship comes in around George. His boyhood friend Sam Wainwright becomes a millionaire, and his brother, Harry, gets the Congressional Medal of Honor. Everyone's life gets defined by money and medals while George Bailey languishes in obscurity, making risky loans to his blue-collar friends.

Then Uncle Billy does the unthinkable. Maybe it was his absentmindedness coupled with his fond affection for Jack Daniel's. Or maybe it was just his euphoria over nephew Harry's major accomplishment. Whichever, he misplaces the bank deposit (right into Mr. Potter's lap) and puts George and the Bailey Building and Loan in the crosshairs of scandal.

It's at this point that the whole movie pivots. George Bailey goes to Mr. Potter and grovels for help but, finding none, decides to end his life so that his life insurance policy can be cashed in to make up the deficit.

Before he can take his own life, however, his plan is foiled by a bumbling angel named Clarence. In the process of explaining his dilemma to Clarence, George makes the powerful statement, "It would have been better had I never been born." So Clarence uses the opportunity to give him a glimpse of what life in Bedford Falls would be like had George Bailey never existed.

The story is powerful and poignant. Clarence the angel shows George that if he had never been born, Bedford Falls would be a much different place. By escorting George into an alternate reality, the angel shows him the sorry state his town would be in if he had never lived.

Without George to rescue him, his little brother who fell through the ice would have drowned instead of growing up to become a war hero who saved his buddies' lives. Without George to stop him, Mr. Gower the pharmacist would have accidentally poisoned an innocent child, lost his license, gone to prison, and ultimately become the town drunk. Without George to love her, Mary would have become a lonely and repressed spinster. Without George to stand up to him, Mr. Potter would have embedded his greedy claws into the heart of the town, strangling it economically and turning it into a sad reflection of himself.

George Bailey thought his thwarted life was an abject failure. But the truth is, his life—and especially his reluctant choice to stick it out in the conventional world of Bedford Falls instead of following his lofty dream—gave the town hope and happiness and kept it from sinking into grim despair.

It's a Wonderful Life shows us that every life, no matter how seemingly insignificant, no matter how thwarted in its hopes and dreams, makes a huge difference. Each of us is a potential George Bailey. Our daily decisions and actions have far-reaching effects we will never see. Squirrels hiding acorns in the ground for the winter have no idea that those they forget to dig up will be mighty oak trees decades after they're gone. The little things we do every day either allow or prevent the web-weaving schemes of the Mr. Potters of the world.

Suicide wasn't the answer for George Bailey. Until Clarence opened heaven's window, George didn't realize what an impact his life had—a life he thought was truncated and meager.

In the last scene of the movie, George is surrounded by his wife, his children, his friends, his family, and the customers of his business. All have rallied to save him from despair and financial ruin. At that point he realizes that his Plan B life is worth living—indeed, it's the best life he could possibly have.

2

IT'S NOT ABOUT WINNING; IT'S ABOUT FINISHING

August 1992. Barcelona. It was the semifinals of the men's 400 meters.

From Jim's vantage point, his son looked like a tiny dot crouched in the distance. But in his heart, he was bigger than life. If the people sitting around him in the bleachers had half a clue as to the price Derek Redmond had paid to earn his place in those starting blocks, they'd be giving him a standing ovation in advance.

Five surgeries on his Achilles tendons and months of painful therapy had helped Derek recapture his world-class speed. He had run a 45.02 and 45.03 in the first two rounds—his fastest times in five years. Jim Redmond took one last peek through his binoculars at his son, who was poised for the start, and then held his breath.

At the gunshot, Derek leaped from the blocks and picked up a perfect stride for the first turn. He was around it in seconds. His father eyes were riveted to him as he turned up the retro-rockets for the backstretch.

You would have had to be up close to Derek to have heard the pop. No one heard it but him. But there was no mistaking the agony that twisted his face as fierce pain tore through the back of his thigh. Derek fell across lane 5, squeezing his right leg. His hamstring had snapped.

The crowd reacted with gasps and quick questions to the people sitting around them. "Somebody's down! Who?" Jim knew. His eyes had been trained on his son the whole way. When he saw the team colors of Great Britain hit the track, his heart had sunk. His son was down, and his Olympic hopes were dashed.

Race officials ran to Derek's aid. And then it happened, almost as if it was in slow motion. Jim Redmond saw his son wave the officials away as he rose to his feet. With pain shooting up his leg and contorting his face,

Derek Redmond started hobbling his way for the remaining 220 meters. His goal was no longer gold, but a driving need to finish what he had started.

While Derek was falling forward around the last turn, his father was racing down the stadium steps to the bottom row of seats. Security people and policemen lined the track. Most were watching the crowd, while some watched the drama unfolding on the oval beneath them. A couple of ushers saw Jim climbing over the rails to get on the track. They tried desperately to stop him. They failed. Jim leaped to the field and started running to his boy.

Although the sound of the crowd had been deafening as they applauded this young athlete's determination, for a split second they fell silent as his father finally caught up with him at the end of the turn. Derek grabbed onto his father, leaned heavily on his right shoulder, and started to sob from deep within himself. Jim lifted the weight off his son's right leg. And then, arm in arm, they turned toward the finish line. To the cheers of an entire world, father and son finished the race together.

For the most part, our job as parents is to teach our

children how to run the various races of life and then faithfully cheer them on to the finish. We station ourselves strategically and offer as much encouragement as we can. But every once in a while, something happens that our children couldn't foresee—they're blindsided by a Plan B setback they never counted on. It takes them down and wants to take them out. That's when we have to be prepared to leap to their aid.

That's what Jairus did. The incident occurred almost two millennia before the Redmonds struggled across the finish line together, but it was no less dramatic. Most people looking at Jairus would have figured him to be a man who knew how to solve his own problems. After all, he wore the designer labels of a high-ranking synagogue official. He had money, education, and connections. But all his wealth and influence couldn't solve his crisis. And his heart was breaking as he reflected on his helplessness.

That's what drove Jairus to the feet of Jesus. The drama is recounted in Mark 5:21–43. As a father of two daughters, I can scarcely read this story without choking up. You see, Jairus had a twelve-year-old daughter who was dying. All of his human options had been exhausted.

He needed to save his daughter's life—that's what propelled him to plead his case to the Savior.

"Seeing Jesus, he fell at his feet and pleaded earnestly with him, 'My little daughter is dying. Please come and put your hands on her so that she will be healed and live'" (vv. 22–23). And with that simple act of faith, Jesus began to make His way with Jairus to the side of his little girl.

They couldn't get there immediately, though. There were crowds of people along the way and in the way—other needs and other crises. It was just after Jesus had given new hope to someone else that the men from Jairus's house intercepted them to break the bad news. "Your daughter is dead," they said. "Why bother the teacher any more?" (v. 35). Like the ushers who tried to hold back Jim Redmond when he came to the aid of his son in Barcelona, these men were trying to explain to Jairus why his efforts were futile.

But Jesus saw things differently. He was in the second-chance business. The Plan B business. That's why He chose to ignore the men and their gloomy outlook on the situation. He said to Jairus, "Don't be afraid; just believe" (v. 36). And with that encouragement tucked deeply within a crevice in his faith, Jairus walked Jesus to his home and watched Him raise his twelve-year-old daughter from the dead.

Do you notice anything that Derek Redmond and Jairus's daughter shared in common? Neither asked for the parent's help. They couldn't. Each of them was too preoccupied with injury and illness to be able to reach out. But that didn't stop their folks from taking action.

Your child might seemingly be down for the count . . .

. . . academically paralyzed with discouragement in college,

. . . hopelessly overscheduled, yet unable to say no to new demands,

. . . enthusiastic about a new opportunity but lacking the skill needed to get over the first few hurdles,

. . . so shaken by the knife of betrayal slipped into his back by a trusted so-called friend that he's stopped believing in himself,

. . . so overwhelmed by her fears that she can't muster the courage to do what she knows she should.

That's when you have to be prepared to leap from your seat among the spectators and come alongside your children—to offer a shoulder for tears and to help lift their burden long enough to get them across the finish line. Maybe they won't cross it first, as they had so dearly hoped. But with you at their side, they can learn that finishing is still possible and still important, even when the glory of standing on the podium has vanished. And when you cross that line, you can be certain that there will be a pair of nail-pierced hands not far away . . .

. . . applauding.

♪ . . . He will exalt over you with loud singing as on a day A Festival !!!

3

THE HEROIC CHOICE
OF LIFE

It was the transition weeks between winter and spring in Fayetteville. Gray clouds, thick sweaters, and an extra blanket at night were reminders to the undergraduates at the University of Arkansas that they still had a ways to go before summer break. But it didn't matter, because it was Friday night—the exclamation point of the week. Razorbacks were rocking and rolling in the weekend at the crowded clubs and bars that dotted the perimeter of the campus.

Cindy was one of the few exceptions. Her best friend and a couple of other girls had been sitting around talking and laughing that night in a tame way that would make their moms proud and their dads breathe a sigh of relief. These were great girls with good heads on their shoulders. At about eleven thirty, one of them suggested they move the conversation to a local fast-food restaurant. That was when Cindy bowed out. She had been fighting a sore throat and needed to get a good night's sleep. As soon as her girlfriends took off, she took a stiff cup of Nyquil and turned in.

That's how Cindy ended up being that rare coed in Fayetteville who was asleep before midnight on a Friday night. She was doing everything about as right as anyone could do it. That's what made the crime committed against her that night so much more bewildering.

She didn't know her attacker. With the darkness of her room, his dark clothing, and the murky fog Nyquil can leave in your head, no one could know. She simply awoke to the full-blown nightmare of a sexual assault. While her friends sipped Diet Cokes and nibbled on fajitas at Taco Bell, Cindy screamed for help. Nobody came to her rescue. Her assailant left as suddenly as he appeared, leaving Cindy shivering with fear in her bed and begging the darkness for mercy.

When the shaking finally stopped, Cindy had to decide what to do. She ended up doing what many rape victims do: *nothing*. She didn't call the campus police. She didn't go to the emergency room. She didn't call her parents. She didn't tell her friends. In her fear, confusion, and despair, she simply went numb.

She might have maintained that state of mind, but circumstances dictated a forced encounter with reality. Less than a month later she noticed that something wasn't normal inside of her, and a trip to her doctor confirmed it. In the late autumn she would be having a baby.

Cindy fell into that small category of people the pro-choice advocates try to use as a justification for abortion. Had she gone to the emergency room the night of the assault, the procedure they would have automatically done on her would have removed the life from her womb. Even after the fact, had she chosen to abort the baby, Cindy would have found plenty of people within the Christian community who would feel she was justified in getting rid of the results of another person's crime.

But that wasn't the way Cindy was raised, and it wasn't the way she felt the Bible taught her to respond in situations like this. She got confirmation on both con-clusions when she finally broke her silence. Her parents, of course, went through the normal emotional reactions any parents would go through. But they processed their rage, their frustration, and their grief at the foot of an ancient cross. Ultimately, they'd have to leave justice up to the Highest Court in the universe and trust God, the Righteous Judge, to deal properly and thoroughly with the evil person who had robbed their daughter of her purity and her youth.

Cindy's parents enfolded their daughter with their love and supported her in her decision to give the baby life. Her dad had always been an outspoken advocate for the protection of human life. Cindy's dilemma put his convictions to the test. He didn't flinch.

When she told her pastor, he wrapped Cindy in the arms of the church and committed the full extent of its love and care to her for the ordeal that she would have to face.

On Mother's Day, while sitting in a pew and listening to Pastor Tom teach from the book of 1 Samuel, Cindy decided on the baby's name. Tom was teaching about the great matriarch Hannah and how she had trusted the Lord through emotionally and socially difficult circumstances. God had heard Hannah's cry and blessed her with a baby. Cindy decided right then that if her baby was a girl, she'd name her Hannah. Hannah was born the first week of January.

The third Sunday in January is Sanctity of Life Sunday. Pastor Tom had made a commitment that until the Supreme Court overturned the *Roe v. Wade* decision that legalized abortion, he would use that Sunday to preach a sermon encouraging the sanctity and protection of the unborn. This was also a Sunday when Pastor Tom traditionally had new parents come up on the platform before his sermon with their newborns to have a special blessing prayed over them.

Tom was in his study, preparing his sermon for that special Sunday. His phone rang. It was Cindy. She wanted Pastor Tom to pray a blessing over her and Hannah before the sermon, and she wanted Pastor Tom to tell her story of how God had given her a beautiful daughter in spite of the horrible crime she had endured. As far as the blessing went, Tom was fine. But as far as telling Cindy's story, everything inside of him said no. It just didn't seem like the right thing to do. Cindy's experience was too sensational, too overwhelming. He didn't want to take advantage of her situation that way.

A couple days later, Cindy called her pastor again. She told him that she felt confident that the Lord was leading her to dedicate Hannah and have Tom tell her story. She urged him to reconsider. He asked her to give him some time to pray about it. Ultimately, he agreed to her request.

People who heard Cindy's story that morning said there wasn't a dry eye in the house. When they listened to Pastor Tom tell of this brave young woman's ordeal and gazed at the precious baby girl sleeping in her arms, they were overcome by the power of the love and the miracle that Cindy and Hannah represented.

One young man sitting toward the back of the church stared in awe. He had always admired Cindy from a distance but had assumed she was married. Now the facts of her story, the testimony of her life, and the little miracle named Hannah were all he could think about. He was determined to shed his social fears and meet this marvelous woman.

Lukas followed his heart. Resolve defeated shyness, boy met girl, love waited in the wings, and eventually, Cindy married this tremendous young man. He adopted Hannah as his daughter. The three of them can be found each Sunday, hand in hand, making their way into church.

God knows how to turn our tragedies into opportunities. He knows how to lift us out of the darkness of some of the deepest pits of our life to let us bask in the sunlight of His grace.

Have you cried out of your despair and wondered if God is even there? Does some dark disappointment hover in the shadows of your day-to-day life, stealing your joy? Do you long for some vindication or reconciliation of your regrets? Don't stop believing. Be like Cindy. When life doesn't turn out the way you expected, do what's right and don't stop trusting in the God who hears your cry.

"Those who hope in the LORD will renew their strength. They will soar on wings like eagles; they will run and not grow weary, they will walk and not be faint" (Isa. 40:31).

4

A DYING MAN'S
ANSWERED PRAYER

His career was legendary. His voice: one-of-a-kind. His cadence: syncopated. For millions of Americans, he was as essential to their daily routine as a good cup of coffee and the sports page. The late Paul Harvey led the pack in sound-bite journalism. His daily ten-minute newscasts were heard by millions, and his famous *The Rest of the Story* vignettes literally rerouted traffic and changed behavior patterns.

I know. He's done it to me. I've sat in my car in the garage (when I was supposed to be in my place at the south end of the dinner table) just to hear the ending of one of his fascinating stories. He was a genius at surprise endings. I'm not. But I'd like to borrow one of the tools from Paul Harvey's toolbox and tell you my own little "Rest of the Story."

Everett was like most dads out there with a houseful of girls. He spent a lot of time feeling outnumbered, cleaning mascara out of his sink, waiting in his car outside of malls, and occasionally finding a pair of panty hose statically clinging to a pair of BVDs in his underwear drawer. But he was different from most dads in the sheer number of hours he spent praying for his girls' futures.

Like most men out there, Everett wanted to make a living for his family and leave a little something behind that would make this world a safer and better place to live. But he was different from most men in that he didn't just desire to make things better; he turned his wishes into actions. He worked overtime to create a home environment for his wife and daughters that would help build them into great women of God. His wife served God faithfully, and his daughters brought them both great joy.

When it came to leaving the world in better shape than he found it, I could use the remainder of this chapter to list all the things Everett accomplished in this regard. But I'm only going to mention one: Everett was convinced in his heart that every baby in a mother's womb had a God-given right to be born.

When it came to his family, Everett had two dreams that he put before God on a regular basis. First, he longed to have the privilege of giving his daughter's hand to a godly man in marriage. Second, he longed for his daughter to put a beautiful granddaughter on his lap. Grand-*daughter*, not grandson. Don't get me wrong here: Everett was not against having grandsons. He would gladly welcome a grandson into the family, but there was something deep in his heart that made him long to be the grandfather of a wonderful granddaughter. So he prayed: specifically . . . consistently . . . confidently. He wanted his daughter to marry a godly man and to be the mother of a precious little girl.

There are a few verses in the Bible that get more press time than others. You know the ones I'm thinking about: John 3:16 . . . Ephesians 2:8–9 . . . Romans 12:1–2. If you asked a group of Christians to list their top ten favorite verses, I'll bet these would end up on most of the lists.

There's another verse, however, that I feel confident would show up along with them. It's Romans 8:28: "We know that in all things God works for the good of those who love him, who have been called according to his purpose."

Everett knew that verse, and he believed it. He also got a chance to see it come true in his own life.

Everett was diagnosed with colon cancer. All cancer is nasty, but colon cancer is one of the worst of the worst. It hides until it's ready to pounce, and when it finally makes its move, it moves quickly. Unless a grade-A miracle took place, Everett would be dead in a very short time. The doctors had talked in terms of months—six, twelve, maybe eighteen.

Everett's lifelong dream of a wedding for one of his daughters and a granddaughter on his lap had not materialized, and the cancer that was quickly and deliberately squeezing out his life made him doubt that it would.

Now comes the rest of the story. Actually, you already know what happened because I told you in the previous chapter. Everett's oldest daughter, Cindy, was the University of Arkansas coed who was sexually assaulted. When a woman is raped, there is a 1 percent chance that she will conceive. Cindy found herself in that micro-minority.

Everett believed that a woman had a right over her own body, but not an unlimited right. Her rights, just like everyone else's, stopped at the tip of another human being's nose. The legal and political position that the United States took on the rights of the unborn broke Everett's heart, and the impact of this hurt caused him to become a grace-based advocate for the pro-life position. In fact, Everett had built his case in a stirring, sensitive, and balanced letter to the local newspaper, so much so that the paper chose to reprint it several times. What makes this fact so amazing is that this newspaper, like most major city newspapers, tends to lean more on the side of the pro-choice position.

Everett brought his daughter home from the university to finish the rest of her prenatal term. There was never any consideration of aborting the baby. Everett practiced what he preached, and his daughter had no hesitation in siding with her dad's convictions. They were, in fact, hers as well. They both knew that convictions aren't convenient. Under Everett's consistent leadership and God's grace, Cindy went the distance and ultimately gave birth to a wonderful and beautiful baby. A girl. Everett's heart swelled with love and pride when he finally held his granddaughter in his lap. One-half of his lifelong dream had been realized.

It was when Cindy told the story about her little girl, Hannah, one Sunday morning in church that Lukas sat up and took notice. You remember Lukas. He was a young man in the church who had admired Cindy from a distance but had assumed she was married. When Lukas heard Cindy share about what happened to her, and when he saw the love that she was giving to the child who had come from her assault, he flipped head over heels for them both. God ultimately wove their hearts together, and they set the date for their wedding.

When Everett stood at the back of the church in his tuxedo, it was hard for him to stand up straight without feeling pain. But nothing was going to rob him of completing his lifelong dream. With his beautiful daughter Cindy's arm through his, he walked his girl down the aisle and gave her hand in marriage to a tremendous young man of God.

Everett died a few weeks later. His pastor, Tom, visited with him just an hour or so before. As Tom left the room, Everett called out to him, "I'm not afraid."

Everett saw his dreams come true before he died because he trusted the God who knows how to turn a person's tears into laughter. Did God cause Cindy to be assaulted in order to answer Everett's lifelong prayer? Of course not! Absolutely not! No way! But God saw fit in His mercy and grace to intervene in the midst of their pain to bring a flower out of parched ground.

The rest of the story for Everett and his family is the same one that can be told for any of us who choose to put our faith in the God who is faithful. Life may be beating you down. You may feel as though you have no place to turn and nothing to hang on to. Don't surrender your convictions and don't relinquish your hopes. The God who turned Everett's tears to laughter wants to do the same for you.

And now you know . . . the rest of the story. Good day!

PART 2
Giving Up the "Want to" for the "Got to"

5

THE PROFESSOR WHO
BECAME A WAR HERO

The handful of tourists to my left didn't notice me or what I was doing. It wouldn't have mattered even if they had. I was about to slip through a time warp and leave them behind, along with their SPF 30 and their digital cameras.

I hunched down on one knee. I closed my eyes. My forehead wrinkled and contorted as I commanded my imagination to work overtime. It took a while, and it took some gritty determination, but sure enough, it happened. At first it was just the distant thunder of cannon fire exploding like muted thuds in the back of my mind. Then I started to pick up the distinct sound of musket fire and the ricochet of bullets among the boulders of Devil's Den down the draw to my left. Something ripped through the trees above and rained shredded pieces of timber all about me. A bugle call, some drummers beating out a cadence, and the neighing of horses added to the crescendo of the battle that was building around me. When I sniffed the gunpowder and smelled the sweat of the men on either side of me, I slowly opened my eyes. And there they were . . . in brave, ordered firing lines, with their muskets at the ready. Their blue uniforms were soaked with perspiration from a combination of the sweltering Pennsylvania heat and anticipation of the fight they were about to experience.

But I wasn't there looking for them, I was there looking for *him*—the slim officer with the vivid blue eyes and sweeping brown mustache, standing off to my right. He was Joshua Lawrence Chamberlain, colonel and commander of the Twentieth Maine Regiment, Fifth Corps, Army of the Potomac. And the hallowed ground on which my mental journey through time was taking place was an obscure knoll outside of Gettysburg, Pennsylvania, called Little Round Top.

A couple of weeks ago, our travels as a family brought us within an hour's drive of Gettysburg. It was an opportunity that I couldn't pass up. I have always been a student of history, especially the history of the United States. The bulk of my focus has been on three particularly historical decades: the 1760s, the 1860s, and the 1960s. My theory is that if you can understand what was happening in America in those three decades, you have the best read on what we are and what we are not as a nation. All three decades were costly, but the 1860s clearly had the highest price tag when it comes to human life.

The apex of the human tragedy of the 1860s would be reached in the first three days of July 1863. That's when more than fifty-two thousand Americans would pay a heavy human price, *fighting each other*, in the battle of Gettysburg. It's called the turning point of the Civil War. If the North had not won this decisive victory, America as we know it would never have had the chance to exist. I realize some Civil War buffs believe that everything pivoted on Vicksburg. I disagree. The North could have lost Vicksburg but still gone on to win the war. Had they lost at Gettysburg, however, it would have been over.

My main attraction to Gettysburg was the opportunity to stand among the memories on Little Round Top. So much of the outcome of the conflict at Gettysburg depended on the success of this particular battle, and so much of the outcome of the battle of Little Round Top depended on the leadership of Colonel Joshua Lawrence Chamberlain. I had read several different accounts of this battle, as well as an enlightening biography of Chamberlain. What impressed me most about him were the character, convictions, and courage that ruled his life. His exploits on the battlefield were not honed in the halls of West Point but among the rocky furrows of his parents' farm back in Maine, around the dinner table with a loving family, and in the study halls of college and seminary.

Chamberlain was not groomed for the battlefield. He had entered the halls of academia, fully intending to spend his life as a professor. War had no place in the picture of his future. Yet he had been taught to take a stand for the things he believed in. And when the Civil War broke out, his convictions about slavery and secession compelled him to put aside his life's Plan A and put everything he was on the line for what he believed to be righteous issues.

It was his unwavering commitment to these convictions that kept Chamberlain charging into the teeth of the enemy long after most men would have turned tail and run. His battlefield record is one of the most outstanding of both sides of the conflict. Fourteen horses were shot out from under him. He was wounded six times. At Petersburg, while leading his brigade in a charge against a superior Confederate fortification, he was shot through both hips. He refused to sit out the rest of the war in the hospital. Hobbling out against doctors' orders, he once again led his men in the crucial battles that would bring an end to the war.

It was in the battle of Gettysburg that he received his sixth wound. Standing atop Little Round Top with his shirt covered with blood, with his panicked men out of ammunition and retreating, he ordered them to fix their bayonets and charge down the hill into the teeth of the advancing enemy. His courage led to a decisive victory that kept the Confederates from rounding the hill and marching unimpeded to Washington.

Just a little less than two years later, General Grant chose Chamberlain to command the division that received the colors and arms of the Confederate army at the surrender at Appomattox. Even at this event, his record stands out above the rest. Normally the victors gloat and the vanquished hang their heads in shame. That's what would have likely happened had anyone else been left in charge. But Joshua Chamberlain was committed to the Lord Jesus Christ. He knew that two of the boldest commands in the Bible are the commands to forgive and be reconciled with the people we care for. The surrender meant these men were once again his American brothers. His heart of compassion compelled him to help restore the dignity of this once-proud army by ordering his division to salute their former enemy. It was an unexpected gift that started the healing process in the spirits of the Southern soldiers.

We need to raise up more Chamberlains, because we have another Civil War brewing in our country. This war, like the first one, is a battle over ideals. But in this conflict, the opposing sides are not oriented by geography. On one side are those who believe that God is. On the other are those who believe that He isn't. One side believes that truth is knowable and morals are absolute as well as nonnegotiable. The other believes that there are no truths and that morals are determined as you go along in life.

The battle lines have been drawn in our communities, our schools, our workplaces, our halls of government, and even in some of our churches. Both sides are struggling for the privilege to write the script for our nation's future. And the spoils of this conflict are all the children who wait in the wings for an opportunity to be led into a better tomorrow.

This won't be a war where guns aim at guns, but where love faces off against lies. Because it is fueled by none other than the Prince of Darkness himself, it cannot be ignored, and it will not go away. But I am confident in the power of the cross, the power of the empty tomb, the power of God's Word, and the power of the Holy Spirit, not only to give us courage but also to give us victory over the darkness.

In the meantime, we must prepare our children to stand tall and, if necessary, to stand alone. Even to the point of giving up their own dreams in order to defend their conviction of absolute truth. Their convictions must run deep, their confidence in God must be second nature, and their faith must be forged from the heat of the attack.

The most successful method of turning those kinds of ideals into reality is to let others see those ideals in us. Character isn't enough; it must be *proven* character (Rom. 5:4; James 1:2–8). May the Lord bless you as you set the pace for any Chamberlains-in-the-making you may influence. Take it from a man who has been inspired by spending an afternoon watching him in action.

6

FOR OUR TOMORROWS
THEY GAVE THEIR TODAYS

The year was 1943. The event was a world at war. The time was Christmas. What everyone wanted most under the tree that year was a little package of hope. For millions of innocent people on every continent, however, there wasn't much to put their hope in. Between the jackbooted Nazi army with its chokehold on Europe and the heartless scourge over the South Pacific by the empire of Japan, there seemed to be so little to be optimistic about.

At a time of the year when hearts gravitate toward home, many people found themselves displaced by the impact of war. Others found themselves confined by the prisons of war. Most were simply transplanted by the demands of war. They were the thousands of young men who just the year before were finishing high school or working in some safe job back in their hometowns. Men with dreams and hopes who were just beginning to prepare for and enter their tomorrows. Now, because of tyrants they'd never met and tyranny they'd never asked for, these young men were thrust into Plan B, preparing for certain battle or guarding a lonely post or sitting in a hole across from an enemy committed to killing them.

This was not the life they had planned. These soldiers' hearts were longing for the safety and comfort of their families. They hurt for the sound of their mothers' voices calling them to breakfast on Christmas morning, and for the touch of their girlfriends or wives to snuggle by the fire on Christmas night. They wished they could see their parents, their siblings, and their friends, and many wondered if they'd ever get to see any of their loved ones again.

It's hard for the average American to imagine what that must have been like. We live in safety and enjoy so much abundance today. But there was an entire generation of

Americans — now nicknamed "the greatest generation" — who knew no such luxury.

Some of you who are reading this know exactly what kind of ache they felt. You have a son or daughter, husband or wife, father or mother stationed at an outpost of some foreign conflict right now. You can identify with the soldier or family member of 1943. You understand the pain of the empty chair at the Christmas supper and the stack of gifts that wait for his or her safe return. But you are the exception, not the rule. In the early 1940s, however, just about everyone felt that pain. We were engaged in a war that reached its tentacles of anxiety into almost every home in the land.

Two men sat down that year to try to capture the longing of the soldier's heart at Christmas. Their names were Kim Gannon and Walter Kent—a poet from Brooklyn and a musician from Manhattan. They wanted to give a voice to the dream that so many soldiers felt as they approached the Christmas season so far away from home. And all of us know what they came up with. Their song is now one of the standards of Christmas. When I hear it, I always think of how it must have sounded back in the

'40s when it was first broadcast. It had to be one of those songs you wanted to hear over and over again, yet it hurt so much each time you did.

Many artists who have recorded this song skip the prelude that Gannon and Kent penned to set up the heart of its message. But this little-sung intro gives context to the verses that follow in a way that makes you truly appreciate the price these soldiers and their families were paying. The prelude tells of a soldier's accentuated longing to be around the people and places he loves so much at this time of year, and even though many miles lie between him and these people that are so close to his heart, he wants them to know . . . "I'll be home for Christmas."

When this song was introduced in 1943 (recorded by Bing Crosby), it struck a painful but tender chord with so many people. A young man was out there somewhere, and he was asking his family back home to go through with their normal plans for Christmas. He wanted them to count on him being there with them when it came time to celebrate. He asks them to decorate the house and the Christmas tree, to put presents underneath it, and, if possible, to have a fresh dusting of snow outside to finish the package. Even though they won't see him there on Christmas Eve when the house is awash in the glow of Christmas, he'll be there in his dreams.

I'm taken aback by how many of these soldiers never actually made it home—not that year or any of the years afterward. Recently I've pursued my ongoing love of history by reading several books about that corridor of time, including the powerful and wrenching account of the six men who hoisted the flag on Mount Suribachi in the battle of Iwo Jima.[1] In reading these books, I've been sobered by the sheer magnitude of the sacrifice these young men made. Yet they were called on not only to be away from their families for Christmas but, for far too many, never to celebrate Christmas with their families again. These young soldiers faced unspeakable horrors, under inhumane conditions, while the rest of the country remained near the comfort of their hearths and in the safety of their tight communities.

So many soldiers never returned. After the battle of Iwo Jima, for instance, the U.S. Marines buried 6,800 of their men on that island. They suffered an additional 19,500 casualties. The few who returned home often left part of their souls behind. Very few came back remotely close to how they left.

A poem carved on a makeshift sign at the entrance of the graveyard on Iwo Jima back in 1945 sums it up:

When you go home
Tell them for us and say
For your tomorrow
We gave our today[2]

If we ignore their sacrifice today, I don't think it's because we don't care about what they did. We just forget to remember. That's why I want to remind us that today in this country we are privileged to pursue our dreams and live our lives because there have been brave people who did not. They did not get to live the lives they chose. Circumstances pushed them in another direction, into a life no one would choose in order that their families, their siblings, their wives and children back home would have a future.

That's why every day is a gift. And now, as so many of the greatest generation are leaving us, never to return, I want to encourage you to take the opportunity to say thanks to those few who are still in your midst. They gave up their Plan A so that our Plan Bs would at least get to be lived out in a context of freedom. They finished what they started, and they fought a great fight.

That's what God did for us, isn't it? The God of wonders and Creator of the universe saw that we all faced an enemy we could not defeat. We were doomed to a destiny we could not change. And so He sent His Son from the glory and splendor of heaven to go to battle for us and to die for us. He sacrificed all that He had for what had to be done. He gave His life so that we could have life, and have it abundantly.

7

STICKING TO YOUR POST

The mold of his remains stands in stark contrast to the others. Most were in various stages of repose. Some wore the face of shock and desperation. Others looked as if they simply lay down and died. More than two thousand didn't make it out of the city before it was too late. But he alone stands out from the crowd.

It was AD 79. At the base of a grumbling volcano sat the city of Pompeii, an upper-crust enclave for Rome's rich and famous. A little more than a decade earlier, it had taken a powerful hit from an earthquake—a seismic warning of its impending demise. This time, only expedience and levelheaded leadership would save the fortunate. As it was, about eighteen thousand made it out alive. But the two thousand who were denied the benefit of a running start told a compelling story of the hopelessness of their final hours.

Let's forget about the citizens for now. Their story has been well told in the rows of books that libraries carry on the history and excavation of Pompeii. I want to focus on the soldiers. For the bulk of the ones stationed there, Pompeii was simply their current billet until their tour of duty was over. It wasn't their hometown; it was just the one they were assigned to guard. The people weren't their families; they were just the ones Rome had left in their care. But when the initial rumblings began in nearby Mount Vesuvius, the orders were handed down and the gladiators were assigned their posts.

Reality dictates the obvious. Human nature is human nature. A volcano erupting in the background and twenty thousand citizens panicking in the foreground make it hard to keep one's focus. The brass in charge of the troops might desire it, but few would expect that conscripts far from home would willingly stick to their posts and do their duty in such a hopeless setting. In fact, many of the soldiers discovered in Pompeii were found chained to their posts.

Then there was this lone soldier: vigilant, focused, and dead. He was found almost two thousand years after the fact, still holding his assigned position, weapon at the ready, unfazed, resolute, and unmoved. I have no idea who he was or where he hailed from. But he's the only one out of all the thousands of people who died in this ancient city whom I actually admire. He gets my vote because he didn't run when everyone else did. He didn't think about himself when everyone else would have. A good chunk of those who got out in time owe him for their lives. And in his death, he teaches us all a lesson for today.

Today, we can hear moral and spiritual threats rumbling in the distance that make Vesuvius look mild. At the foot of these threats sit some people we love. God calls us to duty, to vigilance, and to courage. He calls us to hold our posts and to think about others instead of ourselves. He asks us to surrender our selfish interests and maybe even forgo some of our needs and ambitions.

And no matter what, He asks us not to turn tail and run.

I'm not going to go down the laundry list of the biggest threats facing us today. You should know them by now. If you can't articulate them, then you might want to start running; at least you can save yourself. But if you care about the people left in your charge, I thought you might benefit from the standing orders God has issued to those assigned to guard the perimeter.

In the military, they are known as "The General Orders of the Sentry."[1] I will list them as they are written and then adapt them to our scenario in parentheses:

- To take charge of this post and all government property in view. (While we're on duty, we're to assume a position of leadership, keeping a good eye on everything and everyone in our care.)
- To walk my post in a military manner, keeping always on the alert and observing everything that takes place within sight or hearing. (We're not to be mistaken for the run-of-the-mill. We're in the Lord's service. We must pay attention!)

- To report all violations of orders I am instructed to enforce. (We don't do anyone any favors by ignoring the rules. Circumvented standards are useless and meaningless.)

- To repeat all calls from posts more distant from the guardhouse than my own. (Everyone fares better when we keep the lines of communication open.)

- To quit my post only when properly relieved. (For most, it's just before they embalm you.)

- To receive, obey, and pass on to the sentry who relieves me all orders from the commanding officer, officer of the day, and officers and non-commissioned officers of the guard only. (The next generation will do a lot better if we make sure they know what it takes to do their job well.)

- To talk to no one except in the line of duty. (Beware of those who would distract you from staying focused on your calling.)

- To give the alarm in case of fire or disorder. (Don't worry about sounding foolish. Warn others of the threats. Even if they choose to ignore you, they have no one to blame but themselves.)

- To call the commander of the relief in any case not covered by instructions. (Pray, pray, pray!)
- To salute all officers, and all colors and standard not cased. (God and His Word demand our respect and honor.)
- To be especially watchful at night and to challenge all personnel on or near my post and to allow no one to pass without proper authority. (It might be lonely, and it might be frightening, but God is with you. He'll never leave you nor forsake you.)

"Therefore, my beloved brethren, be steadfast, immovable, always abounding in the work of the Lord, knowing that your toil is not in vain in the Lord" (1 Cor. 15:58 NASB).

You are in the Lord's army. Your life is not your own. When you enlisted, you took a pledge to uphold your Commander's agenda even if it means abandoning your own. You are under orders, and you have a post to defend. But you can be sure that if you are vigilant in your duty, the value of your service, confining as it may seem, will far outstrip the value of whatever you sacrificed in order to stick to your post.

8

I DON'T DO DISHES

I'm not into washing dishes. I'll take out the trash, do repairs about the house, mow the yard, and keep an eye on the kid when my wife has to run some errands. But when it comes to washing dishes, that's not my line. I'm sorry, but I don't do dishes."

He was in his early thirties, tanned, professional looking, and sitting in my office because his marriage was losing "that lovin' feelin'." I had already counseled him and his wife together. I had then talked with her one-on-one, and now I wanted to get the same perspective from him.

It was in his litany about his wife that he had brought

up her running complaint about helping in the kitchen. It bothered her that he wouldn't ease her hectic evening schedule by helping her with the dishes, and it bothered him that she couldn't accept his simple explanation that he "didn't do dishes." His objection to doing dishes gave me a pretty good insight into why this couple's young marriage was already hitting troubled waters.

Everybody has something that he or she doesn't like to do. They get around having to do those things either by getting someone else to do them or by letting them remain undone. The problem is, many of these things we don't like to do are often the very things that are essential to someone else's success or joy.

Maybe you're a mom who doesn't like to clean house, a teenager who doesn't like to do math homework, a manager who doesn't like staff meetings, or a husband who can't stand the feel of his wife's fingers laced between his own. So you don't clean it, solve it, hold it, or squeeze it. And for the moment you feel better. Meanwhile, everyone loses.

The problem goes even deeper. Often the things we don't like to do are rooted in some of the deepest fears of our hearts. We're terrified of speaking in public, so we remain silent at a school meeting while a misguided but vocal parent drives some godless agenda down the throats of the school administration. We're afraid of rejection and reprisal, so we remain mute while a loved one pursues a self-destructive habit. Or we're afraid we might end up looking like a fool, so we refuse to follow a clear leading of God in a particular matter.

Our excuses stack up around us, forming an impenetrable wall between the half-baked persons we are and the unlimited persons we could be. Which brings up an observation I've made over the years: the people who achieve true greatness in their work, their family, and their relationship with God is corollary to their willingness to do the things they don't want to do. It's like running a marathon. The people who finish strong are those who consistently laced their shoes before dawn and jogged into the cold and rain while the no-shows and quitters were hitting the snooze button.

At the root of the problem is this: for most of humanity, pleasing the self is Plan A. Almost always, it's a plan that is at the direct expense of other people we should love more. I'd like to suggest that you abandon that plan. Forget the notion of "what's in it for me?" long enough to focus on the most powerful engine of the truly great. In fact, I'd suggest that you dump the "what's in it for me?" notion altogether. Although it's proven to be the drug of choice for a narcissistic society, it has also proven to be one of the great destroyers of long-term relationships.

Selfishness skews a person's ability to reason clearly. Those who abandon that motivation find very quickly that it doesn't hold a candle to the power they harness when they switch to a "what's in it for them?" mindset. It's a consistent "others" orientation that moves our actions from mundane and mediocre to powerful and transformational.

Don't take my word for it; listen to what Jesus said: "Whoever wants to become great among you must be your servant, and whoever wants to be first must be your slave—just as the Son of Man did not come to be served, but to serve, and to give his life as a ransom for many" (Matt. 20:26–28). He pounded His point home a couple of chapters later when He said, "The greatest among you will be your servant. For whoever exalts himself will be humbled, and whoever humbles himself will be exalted" (Matt. 23:11–12).

All I'm talking about here is what God's grace looks like covered in our own sweat! And we know exactly what it takes to receive everyday grace from God. He tells us so in the Bible. James 4:6 says, "But he gives us more grace. That is why Scripture says: 'God opposes the proud but gives grace to the humble.'"

Humility! It's that swallow-your-pride-and-stop-holding-on-to-your-selfish-agenda, others-oriented mindset that the apostle Paul said is the bottom line of people who cast their lot with the Savior. He wrote, "Do nothing out of selfish ambition or vain conceit, but in humility consider others better than yourselves. Each of you should look not only to your own interests, but also to the interests of others" (Phil. 2:3–4).

So you may not like to do dishes, or housecleaning, or diapers, or math homework, or to hold hands. And if you choose to let your dislikes or fears rule the day, you'll get to enjoy comfort or safety. But you'll be a mere shadow of what you could have been, and the people close to you will lose out because of it. I'm grateful that . . .

. . . Noah didn't say, "I don't do floods."

. . . Joshua didn't say, "I don't do Jerichos."

. . . David didn't say, "I don't do poems."

. . . Daniel didn't say, "I don't do lions' dens."

. . . Joseph didn't say, "I don't do adoptions."

. . . Paul didn't say, "I don't do mission trips."

And I'm most grateful that Jesus didn't say, "I don't do crosses."

PART 3
Loving and Leading the iPod Generation

9

PARENTS AND THE
DARK KNIGHT

A desperate cry for help beams across the night sky, reflecting off the face of churning clouds. Gotham is at the mercy of an unyielding evil. The people in charge have run out of ideas. Their only hope is a vigilante who lives in the shadows, wears a mask, and looks like a bat.

There's a reason that the movie in the Batman franchise titled *The Dark Knight* broke box office records when it was released in 2008. It's a metaphor. In this movie, Gotham has been overrun by organized crime. The district attorney has decided to get tough. But he has to work with a police force that struggles with internal corruption. He's not sure who he can trust. Fortunately, he's been aided by the uncorrupted presence and power of the Dark Knight.

Just when it looks as though organized crime is about to be brought under control, a new evil makes its presence known. This evil is not about organized crime; it's about chaos—an irrational bedlam that wants to draw everyone to the lowest, most sadistic and self-destructive level possible. This evil presents itself as the diabolical Joker with his poorly applied clown makeup over his visibly scarred face. His countenance reflects the twisted heart that drives him.

The Joker is the walking, breathing, logical conclusion of the system of thought that is convinced that morals are relative and life is meaningless. "I choose chaos," the Joker confesses. He describes himself as the dog that chases the car. He admits he wouldn't know what to do with it if he caught it: Steer it? Joyride in it? Run over someone? What difference does it make? It's all meaningless.

The Joker is a Hollywood caricature of what the great prophet Isaiah warned would be a reality within the ongoing human drama. Isaiah said, "Woe to those who call evil good and good evil, who put darkness for light and light for darkness, who put bitter for sweet and sweet for bitter. Woe to those who are wise in their own eyes and clever in their own sight" (Isa. 5:20–21).

To drive home the perverted consistency of his irrational evil, the Joker douses a wall of cash with gasoline and ignites it, lest anyone think he is doing his evil actions for personal gain. As Alfred, Batman's valet and mentor, summarizes, "Some men aren't looking for anything logical; some men just want to watch the world burn." And this is where the moral complexity of this movie speaks to us all.

Our children are growing up in an era where the lines separating right from wrong—good from bad—are poorly drawn and often moved at a whim. And there is a consistent public pushback toward people who attempt to mark these boundaries in stone or frame the truths they represent in absolute terms.

Yet even the most misguided among us instinctively knows that love is preferable to hate, compassion beats indifference, freedom trumps tyranny, and brotherhood is better than prejudice. If you dare step forward to advocate these values, however, you quickly realize that they are not collectively embraced by our culture. The contrary voices that rail against absolute truth are especially loud when our love and compassion for the weak and defenseless drive us to denounce evil. In today's culture, it's not tolerant to denounce anything except intolerance toward the chaotic mantra that "anything goes." The contrary voices resist truth's influence and tyrannically support the voices that oppose us.

Which is why I suggest that all of us could learn a few things from this comic book metaphor known as Batman. He is the only superhero who has no superpowers. He isn't made of iron or able to throw spiderwebs around his opposition. He's just a man driven to leverage all his resources for the good of others. Sure, Batman has vast financial assets that enable his handlers to design kitelike wings that let him glide through the night sky and beef up his car with sophisticated technology that empowers him to catch up with the threats. But once he's face-to-face with evil, it is his sheer, incorruptible love that thrusts him into the middle of the fight.

Some try to make Batman into a Christ figure. I'll admit that he's good, but he's not that good. There is someone he resembles much more. It's a dad or mom so reprogrammed by God's grace and formatted by His love that he or she will stand up on behalf of others regardless of the personal price that might have to be paid. These are parents whose Plan A would be to subcontract all of this moral and spiritual heavy lifting to seminary-trained professionals at their church or parochial schools. But they choose instead the Plan B path that calls them to do the right thing even though it's unpopular and to hold to absolute truth even though it comes at great sacrifice. They also know that it's not uncommon to be unappreciated by the very ones for whom you are sacrificing your life.

Toward the end of *The Dark Knight* we are told, "Gotham needs a hero with a face." It's true. And so do our children. They need adults who don't wet their fingers and hold them to the winds of collective opinion before they tell you what they believe. They need uncompromised pacesetters up close to them who believe in . . .

. . . the pure goodness of God,

. . . the systematic order and reason behind creation,

. . . and the eternal potential that lies behind every human face.

They need people who are willing to stand up for these values at the expense of their very lives. Hollywood likes to refer to these people as superheroes. God simply calls them parents.

10

IVAN THE VACANT

People make certain purchases that should come with a "risk factor" tag on them. At least that's what I was thinking when our oldest daughter, Karis, came home with her acquisition. He bounded through the front door, jumped up to lick Darcy's face for a split second, noticed the expansive back yard, and raced through the kitchen toward the green grass—only to bounce off the glass patio door that he obviously didn't see closed in front of him. It was about this time that our cat came around the corner to check out the commotion, saw the black and white spots on unsteady legs, and went airborne, burying every claw he could find into the back of Karis's new purchase.

That was our introduction to Karis's Dalmatian puppy, Ivan. She found him at the dog pound and obviously paid too much for him. He was sleek, aristocratic, and filled with an almost nuclear level of energy. She named him Ivan because she thought he looked regal and Russian. As she saw it, he had czar written all over his perfect face.

Russia had several czars named Ivan. There was Ivan the Great and Ivan the Terrible, but there was another Ivan who didn't get as much ink as his relatives. He lacked some basic skill at the intellectual level. For the most part, they kept him out of sight and didn't let him make any major decisions. One of our kids' history teachers liked to refer to him as Ivan the Vacant. He simply wasn't all there.

This is the Russian czar who comes to my mind when I watch Karis's dog in action. He means well. He appears to love unconditionally. He's completely focused on the people around him. But, for the most part, he's clueless.

Case in point: Karis had gone to the grocery store and

wisely chose to leave Ivan at home. He loves to ride in her car and hates being left behind, but the nice people at Albertson's don't want to see what the meat department would look like if this dog tried to help Karis shop. When she got home, she had to make several trips to the kitchen before all the groceries were in. Ivan raced out to her car and climbed behind the wheel in anticipation of the trip he was certain was awaiting him as soon as she got all of the groceries in the house. Karis wasn't planning any such trip. But she figured her dog was so dim that just leaving him shut in her car while she made her trips back and forth would give him the idea that maybe he'd actually gone somewhere.

Karis shut the passenger door and started to lug a couple of bags into the house when she heard a familiar "click" coming from her car. She turned around to see Ivan with one paw on her dash and the other on the armrest. That's the one that apparently pushed the automatic lock button. Karis dropped the groceries and raced to her car. Sure enough, there was her goofy dog, wagging his tail, licking the windows like an idiot, all the while locked inside her vehicle.

He sat down on her purse—it was in the middle of the front seat—his skinny little hips resting right on top of her keys. Naturally, it was her only set of keys since she recently purchased this car and hadn't been by to have duplicates made.

And so began a comedy of errors that would rank up there with some of the best scenes from *Dumb and Dumber.* She called two friends who are supposed to know how to get cars open without keys. They fumbled and bumbled with a series of coat hangers, exasperated enough to suggest getting a hammer and just smashing open the window. They even tried enticing Ivan close to the door lock with his paws by holding doggie treats up next to the window. He wasn't biting. For him, it was just another adventure involving a lot of new friends and getting the kind of personal attention he loves.

But all along, Karis was aware that this could turn into a crisis. She checked out locksmiths in the Yellow Pages. A few calls gave her a range of how much it would cost to bring in a pro to open the door. It was more than she paid for the dog! But she was prepared to do it if she had to.

In the meantime, her friends still believed they could get the door open. And, eventually, they did. Ivan leaped out, jumped on Karis to lick her face, and then bounded into the house as if nothing unusual had happened.

In this process, Karis got a crash course in Parenting 101. That incident with Ivan the Vacant reminded me of many occasions when our children unwittingly locked themselves in and us out of their emotions, their spiritual life, their relationships, their plans, and their dreams. It's part of the ongoing give-and-take of a family. In fact, Ivan sometimes reminds me a lot of Karis (I don't mean "vacant"—she's actually quite brilliant). She takes on life so enthusiastically that, to her, it's just one long, ongoing adventure. Sometimes, however, she unwittingly turns an adventure into a dilemma by hitting the automatic locks that put her on the inside looking out at parents with coat hangers on the outside looking in. This is when my wife and I give each other those sidelong glances that tacitly say, *How did we ever get ourselves into this?*

The obvious answer is that love got us into this. We could have had a smoother life without any Ivans. We could have done as other couples do, forgone the demands of parenthood and invested our lives in a quiet and closed existence that life without children offers. It's the choice of many, and maybe it works for them. The bumbling boneheadedness of Ivan the Vacant (and children that act like him) may not be what I would have preferred to contend with on a daily basis, but it's better, livelier, more exciting, and more fulfilling than the alternative.

The love that got us into this is the same love that's gotten us through it. And it's the same love that will sustain us through the future. We've learned that if you can keep your head on straight, not overreact, and maintain your sense of humor through the process, the "vacant" times that come with children make us all just a little better.

11

MY CRIMINAL RECORD

It's hard to figure out exactly how you can take a decade or so of character training and blow it all in one afternoon, but I managed to do it.

I was thirteen. It was winter. The backwaters from the Chesapeake Bay had frozen around some of the boats still moored at the public pier in our inlet. Biting wind blew across the frigid water and burrowed deep into our bones. It was a time when kids were holed up inside, restless, bored, and longing for the thaws of early spring and the prospects of summer's heat.

I was one of those kids. January showed no promise of

surrendering its grip on the elements, and seventh grade showed no promise of getting any more interesting. I was standing on the threshold of manhood but still thinking with the irresponsibility of a child. And apparently I had a little more time on my hands than I knew what to do with.

I can't remember who came up with the idea. It doesn't matter. Whether you're the architect of the crime or merely an accessory, it doesn't make your actions any less stupid.

The plan went something like this: One of the summer cottages in the woods by the tidal basin had a slot machine in it. My friend and I knew this because in the summer we had been in the cottage, playing with the owner's kids, and had dropped a few nickels into the machine. The cottage wasn't winterized and was therefore boarded up and secured for the off-season. The slot machine, however, was still there, and the electricity was still on. We figured that if we could fiddle with the lock and get in, we could have a little fun playing the machine.

The lock turned out to be a piece of cake. We didn't have to break anything to get it to turn. Once inside the house, we simply opened one of the blinds to get enough light and plugged in the slot machine. To prime the machine, we had taken all the money we had between us, cashed it into nickels, and stuffed the change into our pockets.

So we spent the next half hour playing that machine. Every few nickels, a cherry would appear and the slot machine would burp out some change. It was a blast. We took turns. My friend would drop in a nickel, pull the lever of the one-armed bandit, and watch the tumblers in anticipation. After a couple of nickels, I'd take my turn. Back and forth the two of us went—losing, winning, losing, winning—until finally the machine held all of the nickels we came with plus all of the nickels of its own it had used to tease us to keep playing. From the time we made our way to the cabin to the moment we ran out of money was barely half an hour.

Once the thrill of the game was over, the fear of the situation hit us. We figured we'd better get out of there before someone noticed something suspicious. We unplugged the slot machine, closed the blinds, and locked the door behind us as we left.

The county cops were waiting for us as soon as we came around the bushes on the side of the house. Apparently, someone had seen us snooping around the cabin and had called the police. We didn't try to run. It would have been futile anyway; they knew who we were because they knew our parents. They immediately separated us and started asking questions. It was not a pretty moment.

The cops got on their radios to get calls out to our parents. They connected with my friend's father first. He was a state trooper. When they explained what we were doing and how we had been caught in the act, he told them to send his son home and he promised to deal with him. My friend took off for home immediately. Which left two county policemen and me. They finally connected with my father. I could only hear one side of the conversation as they explained the details to him. I could tell from their next statement that Dad had apparently asked them what they do with kids who do stupid things. They explained that there was a "process" they put first-incident juveniles through up at the county station, and then they released the kid back to the parents later in the evening. It wasn't technically an arrest, but they didn't tell me that. What it turned out to be was a well-practiced collusion between them and the judge, designed to scare the ever-loving daylights out of young, stupid kids. Dad told them to "process" me and then give him a call when they wanted him to pick me up.

The process was basically a combination of having you sit for long periods of time, with nothing to read, while police walk by and stare at you or grunt and shake their heads or whisper to one another as they look over at you. Then they make you sit next to their desk while they ask you a bunch of questions about your whereabouts over the past ten years when certain unsolved burglaries, car thefts, and murders took place. Then they make you sit some more while they do their stare, grunt, and whisper thing again.

It was very effective. I felt like pond scum and was scared out of my mind. Finally, around nine o'clock that night, my father came and picked me up. On the drive home, he outlined the consequences that he and Mom had thought up for me while I was at the police station.

The final part of the "process" happened about a week later. I had to appear before a judge to find out what they were going to do with me. The owners of the house left it up to the police to do whatever they wanted since nothing was damaged and the war chest inside the slot machine was a little deeper as a result of our visit.

The judge. Let's see now . . . how would one describe what he did to me? Actually, I can't easily give you a feel for what he did because the most effective words to use aren't usually found in writings of Christian authors. But if I dared use them, you'd smile and nod your head and say, "Yep, Tim, got your point. I know exactly what he did to you." I was the last person to appear before the judge that day. Only a few people were still in the courtroom. When they called my name, I mentioned to my dad that it was our turn to go up to the front. He informed me that it was my turn to go up to the front. He'd wait right where he was. He'd be there either to take me home when it was all over or to visit me if they carted me away.

So there I stood, skinny and scared before His Honor. He looked at a report in front of him and then stared at me for a long, long time. Then he ripped into me with a vengeance. His voice exploded. He spoke of the shame I had brought to myself and my family. He talked of my school training, my church training, and how disap-pointed he was that after all that had been given to me in the way of love, and all that had been done for me in the way of character training, that I would respond with this kind of stupid behavior.

After he was done humiliating me, he proceeded to tell me what he would do to me if I ever did anything as stupid again. I'm convinced that my dad put him up to this because they both seemed to enjoy the whole ugly scene a little too much. He ultimately said that he would not place charges against me and released me to the cus-tody and care of my father.

And that's the extent of my criminal record. I never did anything like that again.

What about my friend who got sent home to his father, my friend who never had to go through the stare, grunt, and whisper process, my friend who never had to stand before His Honor and get verbally pistol-whipped? Well, my friend has ended up in an East Coast peniten-tiary twice. He had a dad who had an image to protect—a father who decided to sweep the incident under the carpet and pretend it never happened so that he could protect his own reputation as a state policeman. And because of it, my friend never really got to know what it was like to be a real man.

Bottom line: don't circumvent the negative consequences of your children's foolish actions. If you do, you only set them up for greater heartache. Kids do stupid things. They embarrass us. They let us down. They defy all of our efforts in building their character. When kids do these things, we parents have a responsibility to deal with them in such a way that the consequences of their foolishness come down on their heads hard enough to knock some sense into them.

My father could have let me off with a simple lecture. It would have been easier. But he took the harder, higher road. He loved me enough to let me feel the full extent of my actions. He hated the thought of me making crime a passion more than he hated the personal embarrassment he'd have to endure in church when word got around that Howard Kimmel's son, Tim, happened to be a jerk. And I'm a better man for it.

12

THE VALENTINE'S DRESS

My oldest daughter, Karis, called me at work. Her voice was filled with excitement and anticipation. "Daddy, I just got back from the mall. I found the perfect dress for the Valentine's party at school, and it's marked down to thirty dollars! I have fifteen dollars, and I'm babysitting this Saturday night, where I'll be making the rest of the money I need. If you would loan me the balance, I'll pay you back Saturday night."

My first thought was, *Since when did Karis start buying her clothes?* Then I recalled that my wife had told her that if she didn't want to wear one of the many outfits that were already hanging in her closet, she could get something else, but she would have to purchase it with her own funds. My second thought was, *Since when can you get a party dress for thirty dollars?* When I asked Karis that question, she explained that it was a clearance sale.

I told her that I would spot her the money, and she could pay me back the following weekend. She thanked me and then said she wanted to hang up so she could call her girlfriend and make plans to go back to the mall the next day to get the dress.

The next day, Karis arrived home from the mall at the same time I was getting home from the office. She waved good-bye to her friend and came up to greet me in the garage.

"I got it, Daddy!"

"Great. What did you get?" I hadn't a clue what she was referring to.

"My Valentine's dress."

"Great." I still didn't have a clue. Then suddenly my mind reversed its memory tape to the day before and the phone conversation we'd had.

When we got in the house she said, "I'll go upstairs and put it on to model it for you."

"Great." But as she ran up the stairs, I noticed she was carrying a bag about the size of the one they put in the pocket in front of you on an airplane. I was looking for a big box, or some long, flowing dress on a clothes hanger inside a plastic sheath. Concern started to build.

I was sitting at the kitchen counter reading the mail when she came in wearing "the dress." She was beaming ear to ear with pride, and her eyes studied me for approval. I looked at the dress, then I looked back to her eyes. Then I looked at the dress again and said, "I can see why you wanted that dress, because you look fantastic in it. It's cute, and so are you."

She went on to tell me about looking at a lot of different stores, and how she fell in love with the dress as soon as she saw it. I wasn't hearing much of what she was saying because there was a war raging in my head. It was true that the dress looked great on her, but it was also true that it wasn't much of a dress—literally.

Karis is built just like her mom—tall and statuesque.

The junior high guys who would be attending the party would have enough problems with their hormones without adding what this dress would do to them. But I didn't want to break my daughter's heart.

I knew why she wanted a dress like that. It was the kind that a lot of the girls were wearing. I remembered picking Karis up at the Christmas dance and noticing many of her friends wearing dresses that were next to nothing—skimpy, tight-fitting outfits that would do nothing but complicate the hormonal battle already raging in so many of the guys. I also remembered the thought that crossed my mind when I saw their dresses: *Where in the world is that girl's father? Is he sleepwalking through her teenage years?*

Our teenagers need bold leadership when it comes to making these kinds of choices. And we definitely have to be prepared to challenge the social status quo. We all have to remember that the world system doesn't have to stand in front of God someday and give an account for our children. We, however, do. And as a parent, I realized a long time ago that I must challenge the world's thinking when it comes to the best interests of my kids.

I also learned a long time ago that even if everyone in the world embraced a bad idea and thought it was a good idea, it would still be a bad idea. And Karis's dress was a bad idea.

"Karis, honey, your dress is cute, but I have just one problem with it. You see, dresses are supposed to be high at the top and low at the bottom. Somehow yours got turned upside down." I went on to explain a little about how junior high boys, even conscientious ones, are wired.

I could see her countenance fall. She had already pictured herself wearing that dress at the party, and now her old fossil of a dad was about to ruin her plans. She defended why she thought it was okay, and I let her voice her views. Then I suggested that we think about it for twenty-four hours. Rescheduling these kinds of difficult decisions often gives time a chance to bring reason and balance into both sides of the conflict. I wanted to make sure that I was being reasonable, and I wanted Karis to have time to consider my concerns.

The next afternoon I called her from the office. "Karis, did you get a chance to think anymore about the dress?"

Her response nearly knocked me out of my chair. "Dad, I really like the dress, and I would really like to keep it, but I decided to do whatever you want me to do and not complain about it."

My assistant at the office had to jump-start my heart. I couldn't believe what I was hearing. My daughter is just as capable of giving me a verbal run for my money as yours is, so I was surprised and delighted.

I told her how much I appreciated her great attitude and that it would help a lot in the position I felt compelled to take. In spite of how much she liked the dress, I wanted her to take it back. "But," I said, "I'll go with you to the mall and help you find the perfect dress for the occasion, and whatever it costs, I'll buy it!" She was willing to bend, so I thought I should be just as willing.

As it turned out, Darcy took her to the mall and they found a gorgeous dress for the party. We nicknamed it "Plan B." It complimented her perfectly without compromising her unnecessarily.

As I've said many times before, there's little that's convenient about being a parent, but there is a ton of reward. Our teenage children need to be able to make a lot of their own decisions, but we have to retain veto rights when they make a choice that we feel genuinely jeopardizes or endangers their well-being. We've got to be courageous, and we've got to be firm. There may be tears, and we may have to hear some unkind things said about our decisions. Don't let those things keep you from your resolve to fight the hard battles. If Jesus had caved in to popular opinion, none of us would be saved today.

As parents, it's critical that we do three things and make them highly visible before our kids. First, we must define our convictions. Second, we must not be wishy-washy about them, but etch them in stone. Third, we must gracefully enforce them. Our kids may not like everything we enforce now, but they will like themselves much better in the future if we model before them and instill in them strong convictions to live by. It's a strategy that's short on criticism, long on patience; small on lectures, and big on grace.

PART 4
Experiencing Pain and Loss
Where Grace Grows the Deepest

13

A VISIT FROM HEAVEN

It was New Year's Eve in central Tennessee. It had been a silent night. It was a quiet dawn. Morning's first rays slipped across the living room floor and climbed up the Christmas tree. Prisms flashed from crystal ornaments and bathed the room in rainbows. The Madonna stared down at her baby in the Nativity scene hanging halfway up the tree. "God with us"—it would be a day that could use the reminder.

Jake was the first to stir. He was barely two . . . just old enough to peel a banana and operate a remote control. He was watching cartoons when his dad came to get him ready to head to town. Dave had a big day planned. Today he was going to cut a ton of firewood, but he needed to get his chain saw sharpened first. His wife, Anne, was still asleep, and he had peeked in on baby Jeannie. *Keep the house quiet,* he thought. *Let Jeannie and Anne get some extra sleep.* Dad and son took off to McDonald's for an Egg McMuffin, leaving the girls to their early-morning dreams.

The rope that tethers life to eternity frays when we least expect it. Invariably, it starts to unravel just about the moment we're taking it for granted. While Dad sipped coffee and visited with his boy at the Golden Arches, a lifeline at home was shredding apart. Anne sensed something was wrong when she opened her eyes and looked at the clock. How could she sleep this late without Jeannie waking up needing to be fed? Robe. Slippers. A race to the nursery.

When she stepped up to Jeannie's crib, she knew something was terribly wrong. The baby's blankets covered her lifeless body, and when Anne pulled them down to look at her, it was obvious that she was gone. At that moment, Jeannie's spirit was winging its way to heaven, leaving behind the home she had lived in for a brief three months.

Anne ran out onto the front porch and broke the silent, still morning with her scream: "Help!" She could just as easily have screamed "Why?" Their home was so far out in the country that no one could hear her.

When Dave and Jake turned down their driveway on their return from town, they were shocked to see the ambulance in front of their house. As he gunned it toward the house, the fear and confusion were intensified by the silhouette of a state trooper's vehicle filling his rearview mirror. And so began the saddest chapter of Dave and Anne's life.

It was sudden infant death syndrome (SIDS). No doubt you've heard of it. But until you've gone through it with someone up close, it's hard to process the impact and devastation it has on a family. Anytime a family loses a child, it's tragic. But the subtle benefit of a child dying in an accident or from a disease is that you at least understand what caused the death. That knowledge can assist your grief when it finally comes time to put closure on your loss. The problem with SIDS is the mystery that surrounds it. It not only puts the question *WHY?* in all capital letters, but it also leaves you second-guessing everything you've ever done with, for, or to the child.

Dave and Anne were no exceptions to this pattern of second-guessing. In the days and weeks that followed the funeral, they were paralyzed not only by their pain but by their doubts as well. It took the best experts in the field and the best friends they had to convince them the loss of Jeannie was not a result of their neglect or mistakes. It just happened. No one knows why.

Jeannie's room became an obstacle to Anne's grief. Because of its location, she had to pass by it several times a day. At first, the room simply remained empty, crib and furniture stored away, door shut. Then it became a storeroom for items that people donated to Anne and Dave for an auction they held to raise money for SIDS research. Antiques, a record collection from their neighbor, and various other items occupied it for several months.

After the auction, Anne decided that it was time to live in that room again. Leaving it a mausoleum to the family pain wasn't serving Jeannie's memory. Some fresh paint, some nice art, a box full of toys, a rocking chair, a shelf of children's books, and a love seat where the crib used to stand made the room a great place for Anne and her son, Jake, to spend time together during the day.

It was afternoon. Anne was sitting on the love seat, finding it difficult to get comfortable because of her enlarging abdomen. Her next child was in her final trimester. She would be born in a few months. Jake was sitting next to his mom, listening as she read him a story.

When it was over, they both sat quietly for a moment. Little minds run wild in vast forests within the imagination. Jake had been thinking, wondering, figuring. Somehow, he had been under the impression that Jeannie was still at the hospital. Anne gently explained to him again that Jeannie had died—that she was with Jesus. But he was still confused. He didn't understand how she had died at the hospital.

"Jake, honey, Jeannie didn't die at the hospital. She died here, in this room, in her crib that used to stand where we're sitting right now."

His little eyes looked at his mom and then looked away, trying to sort everything out. Then they got big as saucers, filled with excitement, and his mouth started to form an ear-to-ear smile. "You mean to tell me that Jesus has actually been in this room?"

Click! She could almost hear the tumblers turning in the lock that had bound her pain so deeply in her heart. God had handed her little boy the key to set her free. One simple observation from the uncomplicated mind of a boy who was barely three did the trick. The tears flowed. But they were new tears, different tears, tears of relief, tears of closure, tears of hope. Jesus had been *here.* He had promised that He would never leave them. In fact, He had come personally to give special care to their daughter.

In many ways Anne's story mirrors that of another mom who had a baby. He, too, died suddenly and tragically. She also cried out in pain. She, too, learned what Anne learned that day. She learned it not from a redecorated nursery but from the hollow of an empty tomb that once held the body of her son, whose name was Immanuel, God *with* us.

We all know that life is filled with mysterious hurts that shroud our hearts with doubts. Hopes and dreams are shattered, and loved ones are torn from us. It's in times like these that we need to understand that God has stepped into linear time. He lived a life among us. He paid a price. He bought us freedom from the pains of life and bought us a promise for the joy of eternity. It's because of this that we can go on living and find peace and joy even when our lives seem shattered beyond repair.

Jesus not only *was* in your room; He *is* in it right now. God came to be Immanuel, God with us. And He still is.

14

ANGELS DRESSED IN BLACK

The hot puffs of air turned to vapor around Chuck's head as he jogged back toward his apartment. Brick and steel skyscrapers twisted the crisp breeze off of Lake Michigan into a maze of offsetting currents, updrafts, and biting, contrary winds. It was a tough way to start a day, but when you worked in Chicago, it was the best way to prepare yourself for the tough demands of its marketplace. Chuck braced his chin down closer to his chest and leaned into the wind. As he ran the last quarter of a mile to his building, his mind ran down the list of contacts, appointments, and phone calls that needed to be made as soon as he got to work.

His wife and children were still asleep two time zones away. They weren't on his mind. They hadn't been for a long time.

The blow came from somewhere within the long shadows made by the flat rays of the dawn. Point-blank. Powerful. Delivered with pinpoint accuracy. It crushed in the side of Chuck's skull and put his lights out. It also snapped his head so severely that it smashed the third vertebra at the base of his skull. Chuck's legs crumbled beneath the force of the blow and his momentum hurled him headfirst down a cement stairwell into the basement landing of the Hyatt Hotel in downtown Chicago.

Sometime the next day, his mind stirred from deep within a black hole of unconsciousness and allowed him to detect the beeps and muted groans of the life support equipment that surrounded him. But it was several days later before he understood he was wearing the head halo of a broken neck victim and was going to be a long-term resident of the ICU at Northwestern Hospital and the

Chicago Rehabilitation Institute. It took even longer to piece together the events that put him there.

It was amazing that Chuck was in the hospital instead of the morgue. A false alarm turned in two minutes before his attack brought fire trucks racing to the curb next to the stairwell moments later. It was only because of the height of the fire truck and the fact that some of the firemen were actually riding on top that they were able to see the man lying in the pool of blood at the bottom of the stairs. They immediately called in a paramedical team from the fire station a block away. It was a good thing, because Chuck had received the feared C-1 break to his neck. This injury stops the respiratory process. If Chuck had not received help within a few minutes, he would have suffered irreparable brain damage.

And so began the restoration of an assaulted man's brain, a broken man's body, and a stubborn man's heart. Sitting across the table from Chuck two and a half years later, it was hard not to think that he was just making this all up. It was beyond belief that a man who had sustained those kinds of injuries could walk, let alone speak coherently, write legibly, or draw the conclusions from the ordeal that Chuck now draws.

I had known Chuck for almost a year, but only casually. He attended a men's Bible study I was teaching every Tuesday morning. I had heard that he had been whacked on the head a few years back, but I had assumed it was your average, run-of-the-mill big-city street mugging that leaves you with a splitting headache and an empty wallet. But when Chuck slipped into the seat across from me at a restaurant that morning to tell me his story, he took me on an odyssey through a life punctuated by repeated acts of personal irresponsibility countered by generous doses of God's grace.

Chuck had been born and reared on the Dakota prairies in the 1940s and '50s by a loving mom and dad. His father was a German Baptist pastor who had found Christ through the ministry of the Pacific Garden Mission of Chicago. Chuck had enjoyed grace on a platter as a child. But sometime during his second year at Moody Bible Institute, Chuck decided he had a better plan for his life than God did. He pitched his faith aside and chased pipe dreams littered with money, influence, power, and self-gratification.

His first marriage didn't last long. His second wife gave him two fine children, but he was so preoccupied with himself and his own ego that she had long since turned brittle and indifferent to him. She was the woman who was far from his side and his heart the morning a blow out of nowhere hurled him to the bottom of that stairwell.

"You know, Tim," Chuck told me, "wives are like trees. Trees need fresh air, sunlight, and water in order to grow. When I came home, I sucked the air out of every room I entered. I kept my wife in the dark, never letting her know what I was up to or allowing her to be a part of my daily life. And I kept her thirsting for affirmation and encouragement. All she heard from me was the whining of an overgrown spoiled brat. I didn't blame her for serving me papers in the middle of my therapy. I had given her no reason to stick by my side."

After being clubbed beyond recognition during a morning jog, Chuck now walks among his fellow men humble and grateful to God for His mercy. He's developed a close and tender relationship with his two kids. He and his former wife are enjoying civil conversations and bright moments together. He's a careful student of God's Word and a faithful encourager of the friends God has surrounded him with. It's all the result of a broken neck that God used to rescue a wayward heart.

I asked him, "Have you been able to forgive the person who cracked you over the head?"

"Oh yes," he replied, "I did it shortly after I learned what happened to me."

I leaned forward in my seat, "So they caught the guy?"

Chuck's eyes danced and he got a slight grin on his face. "No, they never caught him. They have no idea who did it." And then he dropped his voice to a whisper and looked around the restaurant before he said, "I don't think they could have caught him even if they'd been there when it happened. Who knows? He might even have disappeared right after he struck me."

I just stared into Chuck's eyes, trying to figure out where he was going. "You see, Tim, whoever it was did me a favor and brought me back to God. And if it took

God snapping my neck to get my attention, it was better than the stupid path I was going down. So for all I know, it might have been an angel dressed in black. Regardless, I'm a different man . . . a better man because of the ordeal."

I was amazed at Chuck's expression of faith. He had been brutally knocked from his life path, his health shattered and his career ruined. His life was now radically different from his original grandiose plans. And he was thankful for it. His ordeal had put him on the path where he should have been all along.

Later, as I watched Chuck shuffle to his car, I wondered how many times God uses catastrophes in our lives to redirect us from a path of self-destruction. Who knows but that some of our worst moments were nothing more than the work of angels dressed in black, sent from a loving God who cares for us enough to do whatever it takes to get our attention and wake us up to a better way?

15

GRACE FOR THE
GREAT RECESSION

As I write this, a numbing economic winter has fallen on our land. But unlike the normal temperature fluctuations that are part of any thriving economy, there's no sign that this present freeze has any intention of thawing soon.

There's hardly a family that hasn't experienced some frostbite. Savings and retirement accounts languish as the Dow hits new lows and unemployment hits new highs. Across the country, people are driving away from mortgages in cars they can no longer afford. Probably the most telling sign of how bleak things may be is the number of headhunter executives who are out looking for jobs—for themselves!

I can't think of any time in my life when families have been handed such a golden opportunity to represent the heart of God to the people around them. Our homes are called to be the headwaters of God's grace that create channels of blessing to flow through every low spot in our culture.

To support my point, I invite you to leaf to the front pages of your Bible and learn from a man who knew what it was like to be thrown headlong into an economic, relational, and emotional winter . . . without even a coat. His name was Joseph (Gen. 37–50). Let me set the scene for you.

Joseph was a great kid, his father's favorite, a dreamer who was envied by his older brothers. His brothers rejected him, abused him, and ultimately sold him into slavery. He was purchased by an Egyptian official who happened to have a lonely and unfulfilled wife. Joseph spurned her advances. She reacted by falsely accusing him of sexual assault.

Joseph was pink-slipped, unemployed, and thrown

into prison in one fell swoop. Through a series of providential events, he got a chance to use God's insight to interpret a dream for one of Pharaoh's handlers. But he was forgotten in prison for two more years until Pharaoh had a dream that stumped his own wise men.

At that point things moved quickly. Joseph was taken from the prison and given a bath, a shave, and a change of clothing before he was whisked into Pharaoh's presence to see if he could interpret his dream. From this humble position, Joseph heard the dream and then immediately gave its interpretation from God. Egypt was going to experience seven wonderful years of bounty and blessing. But these would be followed immediately by seven years of famine so severe that the Egyptians were going to forget all of the blessings they once enjoyed. Sound familiar?

Now, here's where we need to pay close attention to the story. What happened next revealed the heart of Joseph as well as the true face of grace. Joseph had endured a prolonged season of backstabbing, rejection, humiliation, and pain from his family as well as the Egyptians. He had just heard that God was about to destroy his oppressor's economy and possibly see the bulk of their population die of starvation. Based on the way they'd treated him, it would've been easy for Joseph to be delighted that they were finally getting their just deserts.

But Joseph was ruled by the power, presence, and compassion of God, which gave him an immediate concern for the Egyptians' welfare. Once he explained the meaning of the dreams, his superb problem-solving skills, as well as his sophisticated administrative skills, kicked in as he volunteered a plan that would enable Pharaoh to leverage this news in a way that could save his people. It's what you do when you live your life for others.

You probably know the rest of the story. Pharaoh made Joseph the equivalent of prime minister of Egypt. He gave him a beautiful wife, who gave him two great sons. And these events put Joseph in a position to save his own family from starvation as well as relieve his brothers of the heavy weight of guilt they had been carrying for selling him into slavery so many years before.

The moment the brothers learned that the CEO of Egypt was the brother they had maltreated, they were terrified. They assumed that with his power and their former crime against them, they were certain to be dead men soon. But instead of taking the golden opportunity to even the score, Joseph offered grace:

> "Do not be afraid, for am I in God's place? As for you, you meant evil against me, but God meant it for good in order to bring about this present result, to preserve many people alive. So therefore, do not be afraid; I will provide for you and your little ones." So he comforted them and spoke kindly to them. (Gen. 50:19–21 NASB)

No one's Plan A includes recession. But when economic winters come, they are not excuses to show fear but opportunities to live by faith. Our response can't be strategies that only take into consideration our own survival. These are not times when we lessen our commitment to the spread of the gospel; they are times when we ramp it up. These are not times when we limit our concern for the poor, the lonely, the sick, the helpless, or the hopeless; they are times when our concern compounds manyfold. During economic summers, we give from our surplus. During economic winters, we give from our sacrifice.

These tough times are perfect opportunities to step

forward and speak up with a clear hope; to roll up our
sleeves and get involved in bringing substantive help to
the hurting; and to give people a walking, breathing
example of what God's grace looks like covered in com-
passionate determination. Your commitment to practic-
ing grace in the midst of a harsh economic winter may
be the only warmth the people closest to you will be able
to enjoy.

In economic winters, plan A for most people is to
close the cupboard doors, shut down the charitable giving, and hang on to what you've got. A better plan is to
live more simply, expect less, and give more. And above
all, to trust the One who feeds the sparrows to free your
mind from worries.

The good news is that the coldest winters set up some
of the most abundant springtimes. "Let your light shine
before men, that they may see your good deeds and praise
your Father in heaven" (Matt. 5:16).

16

HER LAST CHRISTMAS

It was Christmas night. Time for bed. The old woman loosened the pins that held up her hair and let it fall down past her shoulders. Her glistening, jet-black locks had long since faded into gray. They looked tired and worn out, just as she did, sitting on the edge of the bed, working her comb through the tangles. As she pondered this quiet finish to her Christmas, she wondered if it would be her last.

Life is seldom easy for anyone, but for some, it's unusually tough. Life had been extremely difficult for her, but she wouldn't complain. She couldn't. It wouldn't be right.

Being a single mom was now part of her past. All the kids were grown and gone. The grandchildren stopped by occasionally, but not as much as she had hoped. And not today. That was okay, though, because as she had grown older she had also grown more desirous of spending Christmas by herself. It helped her make sense out of the confusing events that made up her life.

When she was a little girl, her mother told her that way back in the root system of her family tree she could list some royalty. But somewhere along the line, her family's pedigree had slipped from blue blood to blue-collar. Mom wore the same dress every day, and Dad always wore a cheap cologne called "fresh sweat." They were good folks, though—quiet people who worked hard, prayed daily, worshipped faithfully, practiced the Ten Commandments, tithed every payday, and always seemed to maintain a practical grasp of the big picture.

But she had caused quite a crack to streak across the face of that big picture when early in her engagement she informed her parents she was pregnant. "You can't be!

What were you thinking?" they exclaimed. She tried to explain. But it didn't make sense to them. "This kind of thing doesn't happen to girls who were brought up like you!"

The scene was complicated even more by the fact that her fiancé wasn't the father, and the party responsible for the baby growing in her womb would not be marrying her. What happened next is a long story. Dad pulled some strings, her angry suitor softened and agreed to marry her anyway, and the invitations were sent out.

The baby wasn't early; the wedding was simply late. But at least the baby had a last name and Mom had a man to help her plod through the uncertain future. She and her new husband took up housekeeping and parenthood at the same time.

From the beginning, however, it was obvious that the boy was different. He was the kind of kid who liked to color outside the lines. He wasn't spiteful or antagonistic to his mother and stepfather, but it was apparent from the outset that they weren't going to have the luxury of coasting through his childhood. They would have to pay close attention and take good notes.

His real father established a trust account for him—a peculiar combination of cash and an interest in a perfume company delivered by international agents shortly after he was born. His stepfather didn't hesitate to use it, financing a relocation that was necessary to avert the consequences of the boy's first run-in with the law. It would become a pattern that would dog him all the way to the end of his life.

Siblings came along . . . a couple of brothers, a couple of sisters—good kids, conscientious, a credit to the household. From the outside it looked like a normal home, but if you were privy to the banter around the dinner table, you'd realize that this blended family struggled with some serious sibling rivalry. *Their* kids had a hard time accepting her kid. As far as they were concerned, he didn't fit in. He danced to a different rhythm, had peculiar taste in friends, and had a bad habit of showing them up.

Then her husband died. Too soon. Too young. He had been a good man. She finished the job they had begun together, but alone, a widow, a single mom.

The old woman slipped off her dress, slid into her nightgown, and then went to the sink to run a wet washcloth over her face before she climbed into bed. "I wonder what Jim is doing tonight?" Jim was her second born. He was a pastor down in the capital. Big church. Tons of responsibility. Lots of stress. Both he and J. J., his younger brother, had gone into the ministry. It was hard to believe when you stepped back and studied them against the backdrop of the full picture. From the way they'd treated their older brother, you'd think they weren't qualified to wear the collar and take the call. They had been resentful of him, taunted him, and just about wrote him off. "He's nuts, Mom. He frequents the wrong side of the tracks and hangs around with losers. He's making waves with the powers that be. If he keeps it up, they'll take him down." Their hunches turned out to be right—at least, half-right.

She knelt beside her bed, whispered a few tender words toward heaven, and then climbed under the covers. Reaching over to the nightstand, she took the little cross she always kept there and held it up into the faint light to study its silhouette. It was hard to believe that one woman's life would get to witness this much majesty. And with that thought, she let her mind drift back to her first Christmas, in that stable at the end of the alley.

Joseph had been such a trooper—a quiet and sturdy gift of God, patiently helping her give birth to the Son of God. She closed her eyes to remember the sight of the Savior nursing at her breast—the mystery, the miracle, the message. She thought of the shepherds crowding around the manger—leather-skinned men with callused hands arguing over whose turn it was to hold the King of kings next.

It was the Christmas that set the stage for the crucifixion. It was the Redeemer who validated His identity through resurrection. It was the boy who died for His brothers. It was the God those brothers now served. James, Jude, the disciples, that tireless apostle called Paul. It was indeed too incredible for words.

Of all the women in the nation, how could this have happened to her? Before the angel came with God's offer, she would never have chosen such a life. She could have avoided the sneers and gossip of those who never forgave her unwed pregnancy. She could have avoided the fear and pain of seeing her son arouse the anger of people in high places. She could have avoided the agony of seeing

Him beaten to shreds and hanging to die on that bloody cross.

But looking back, she was so thankful that she had not shrunk back and turned the angel away. It had been a life of pain, but now that the years were tallied up, the joy was far, far greater than anything she could have found in the normal life she had dreamed of as a girl.

She laid the cross back on the nightstand and then leaned over and blew out the candle. Pulling the covers up over her shoulder, she rearranged her pillow and settled on her side. Silent night, Mary, holy night. All is calm, all is bright. Sleep in heavenly peace. Sleep in heavenly peace.

PART 5
Thriving, Surviving, and High-Fiving

17

AND ON THE EIGHTH DAY, GOD CREATED GOLF

I realize there's no solid biblical proof for the assertion of this chapter title, but if someday I get to heaven and find out my hunch was right, I won't be surprised.

Why do I think that? Well, it just takes a few holes of golf before you realize how much you need a Savior. The worst part of our makeup as humans surfaces on tee boxes, the edges of fairways, and two feet from the cup. You can start a round of golf with every intention to play in the Spirit, then you chili-dip a textbook pitch and three-putt from eight feet. The game is tailor-made to put a man in the confession booth for a couple of weeks.

This story isn't about golf. If it were, many of you would stop reading right here. Golf is a game that doesn't enjoy a middle ground with people. The folks who don't play golf either don't understand it or write it off as a silly waste of time. Those who do play fluctuate between love and hate, depending on how well their last shot went. I've had days where it all seems to come together for twelve holes. The last six holes remind me how important it is for me to keep my day job, and one of those six makes me wish I had the power to order an air strike on Scotland.

Why Scotland? In golf mythology, idle Scottish shepherds are blamed for introducing the game. But I believe they were merely carrying out God's creative plan for mankind. God knew we would be arrogant, prideful people, so after getting a day's rest from His week of creating the universe, He said,

"While I'm at it, let there be golf." And there was golf.
And God saw the game that it was good for humiliating full-grown people. And He said, "This is good."
And God divided the game into holes, and the land

into fairways, and the first hole to the eighteenth were the first round. And then God giggled and said, "This shall be a hoot." And it was a hoot.

It's not that God has a sadistic streak. It's that man has an arrogant streak. So somewhere there was a need to remind people who indulge in excessive periods of self-sufficiency that they are, when all is said and done, merely mortals. Thus golf. The old joke goes that it's called *golf* because all the other, more appropriate four-letter words were used up.

You'd think people would have enough brains to walk away from a game so adept at bringing the worst out of them. You'd think that after spending a truckload of money on titanium promises and overpriced lessons only to see your score go up, you would cut your losses and take up napping. But that would assume that the average duffer's intelligence quotient is at least a point higher than his ego quotient.

The fact is, most hackers I know act as if they snacked on lead-based paint chips most of their childhood. Just when you think it's time to give up the game, you get all of a four-iron from 190 yards into the wind and roll it up to three inches from the pin. The proof that you've lost your mind is that you don't do the next logical thing—which would be to race to the nearest convenience store and buy a lottery ticket on the occasion of it being your lucky day. No, we actually mark our ball, wait for everyone to putt out, tap in for the bird (to the praise of all) and then walk over to the next tee and hit our drive into the lake.

I think the addictive allure of golf has to do with the microcosmic parallel between a round of golf and a round of life. In less than five hours, you can take an emotional roller-coaster ride on par with your first six years of marriage. Taking three strokes to get out of a sand trap reminds you how many times you changed your advice to an inquiring teenager before you finally got it right. I had the yips once in a tournament that brought back memories of my first ten years after grad school. That was when I was working overtime to be as good as I could be, only to find that in the huge scheme of life, I was at best mediocre. This isn't false humility; it's unvarnished honesty.

But therein lies the hope.

The reason I keep tying on my golf spikes and teeing up the little white ball is probably the same reason I keep moving on in my marriage, in my role as a dad, and in my work as a professional. I'm not as good a golfer as I'd hoped to be, but I keep playing. I'm not as good a husband as I'd hoped to be, but I keep trying. I'm not as good a father, a speaker, a writer, or a Christian. But the point is that that's not the point. As G. K. Chesterton once said, "Anything worth doing is worth doing poorly." He didn't mean that we should try to do things poorly; he meant that there are things that should be done even though we lack the ability to do them as well as we would prefer.

The important thing is not the scorecard; it's completing the round. It's keeping on walking from one green to the next tee, birdie, bogey, or sand trap. My life is not golf. Nor is my life my wife, or my kids, or my work. The times I've tried to force it to be those things are the times when I've proven to be the biggest disappointment to the people who needed me most. When I just relax and let Christ be my life, my hope, and my joy, it helps me take my focus off my scorecard and disentangle my ego from my handicap. And therein lies all of our hope.

Have you four-putted an opportunity to show grace to your spouse lately? Have you had to take stroke and distance for an untimely word to one of your kids? Did you slice into the rough on a recent project at work? Don't panic. We all slip on our spikes over feet of clay. Those who know and understand this are those who appreciate the Savior most. So humble yourself before the right hand of God, and He will exalt you in due time.

18

HIGH FIVES

Wynnona's voice drifted back into the speakers of my minivan, as Travis Tritt's distinct twang came up underneath it. KNIX, "Arizona Country," was in the middle of fourteen-in-a-row, and if things went the way I hoped, I'd be able to listen to all of them before Karis showed up. I was in the parking lot behind the high school, waiting for the cross-country team to get back from their practice run. I figured Karis was three or four miles off in the distance, sweating her way back toward the locker room. Meanwhile, I could ease my seat back to a more prone position, put my feet up on the dash, hum along with

Garth, Reba, and Clint, and watch the varsity football team practice.

If I could have slipped through a time warp and gone back a couple of decades, one of those guys in the practice jersey and football helmet would have been me. I played high school ball. Back then I loved the game, but I tolerated practice as a necessary evil. Now, in the comfort of my van, I found football practice a lot more enjoyable. Somebody else's pain was my gain. As I sat there watching the guys run through their drills, I realized that practice hadn't changed much over the last quarter century. That's probably because when you distill the game of football down to its basic parts, it is still a combination of blocking, tackling, and falling forward.

But there was one element of the game that had slipped into the playbook somewhere between the time I turned in my helmet and they brought back the two-point conversion. I'm not sure when it became standard operating procedure, but its presence among the players gave this practice a distinctly modern feel.

It was the generous use of the high five. A cornerback would dive toward a wide receiver running a down-and-out pattern, stretch his hand into the play, and knock down the pass. As he jumped up off the ground, the safety would smack him a high five. The quarterback did the same to the fullback, who broke loose for a nice thirty-yard gain.

High five. It's a nonverbal "Way to go!"—a response to a job well done. Both on the field and off, in any and every walk of life, from professionals on down, it has become the universal gesture of approval. Sometimes high fives are exchanged between people who worked as a team to pull off something spectacular. Not long ago at a wedding I was performing, I told the groom he could kiss the bride. He followed my instructions admirably, and then they snapped a high five to the applause of the crowd.

Sometimes high fives are exchanged between people who have nothing to do with whatever got them excited but want to celebrate it anyway—like the people in the bleachers who high-five total strangers because their team just put some points on the scoreboard.

It got me thinking . . .

There are a lot of places in the Bible where a high five

would have been appropriate. For instance, the last of the children of Israel climbs up the steep, dry banks of the Red Sea while the thundering hooves of Pharaoh's army are pounding their way through the path God had cut in the water. Moses stretches out his staff and the walls of water come crashing down, drowning the army. It would have been a perfect place for Moses to turn to his brother, Aaron, and slap him a high five.

How about those three teenagers who stood up to the Babylonian king, Nebuchadnezzar? An edict had been passed saying that when they heard the Babylonian marching band in the distance, they were supposed to bow down to a statue of the king. Noncompliance would mean some pretty nasty consequences. It was either bow or burn. Shadrach, Meshach, and Abednego took their chances with the consequences rather than compromise their convictions. For their courage they got themselves thrown into a fiery furnace. But in that furnace, they were visited by a messenger from heaven who rescued and delivered them. Coming out of the heat and flames of the oven would have been a perfect place to smack some high fives.

Slip up the timeline several hundred years and you catch the shepherds waving good-bye to Mary, Joseph, and baby Jesus, then turning to each other, slapping a high five, and heading back to the fields to watch their sheep and think about what they had just seen.

I love the story in the Gospel of Luke where those guys removed the tiles off a roof in order to lower their crippled friend into the crowded room where Jesus was teaching. From their perch on the roof, looking down through the hole they had made, they saw Jesus heal their friend and tell him to take up his bed and walk. High five on the rooftop!

The list goes on and on: the disciples after Jesus quieted the storm in the middle of the lake; Mary and Martha after Jesus raised their brother, Lazarus, back from the dead; the people lining the way of the triumphal entry; the prodigal son and his dad; Peter, James, and John at the transfiguration; and the two angels outside the tomb when the stone was rolled away. High five? Yes!

Is your life not going just right? Things not working out just the way you planned? If you are willing to take a walk with Christ past the foot of His cross, then pause at the entrance of His empty tomb and embrace the truth that both of these things represent, then God will turn your life into a series of high-five moments. And whether you actually slap these high fives or simply sense them in your heart, He'll make sure you get more than your share of opportunities.

You might be thinking, *Tim, you don't know what I've been going through. If you could see my life up close and walk a few miles in my Nikes, you wouldn't be so generous with your optimism. We've got bills we can't pay, a car that seldom starts, strep throat haunting our kids' bedrooms, a backed-up septic tank, a leak in the roof, scary neighbors, goofy in-laws, a split in our church, a dog that needs to be put to sleep, piranhas in our birdbath, and company that won't leave. Honestly, there hasn't been much to celebrate in a long time.*

Friend, let me encourage you. The Son who hung in the gap for man's sin, who stretched out His arms in a position to enfold us and then let angry men drive nails through His hands and feet . . . that Son who took a deep breath and cried out, "It is finished!" to the applause and

high fives of the heavenly host . . . that same Son, the
Lord Jesus, has surrounded you with high-five moments.
Just look around, you'll see. They're everywhere. Like . . .

 . . . crossing the threshold of your first home,

 . . . feeling your baby's first tooth,

 . . . watching your baby's first step,

 . . . the first time your child makes his bed by himself,

 . . . her first bike ride without training wheels,

 . . . memorizing his first verse,

 . . . her first attempt at bringing you breakfast in bed,

 . . . a job well done with the lawn mower,

 . . . when you step back and inspect the finished prod-
uct of everyone's efforts at trimming the Christmas tree,

 . . . seeing an original sunset every night,

 . . . realizing that if you've got even one good friend,
you're richer than most,

 . . . waking up to a day that involves people, even
strangers, who you can touch with grace.

You see what I mean. High-five moments are all
around us. I know what you may be thinking: *These are
little, ordinary things that happen to everyone all the time.
They are too small, too insignificant to make a dent in the*

problems and disappointments I have to deal with. Ah, but there's the rub! Those little things that happen to everybody are where real life happens. It's when our own plans don't go right—or often when they get in the way—that we get so busy or distracted that we fail to notice the tremendous joy God gives us in the ordinary. That's when we miss out on the very events that God wants to use to bring us joy and keep us on target.

A country classic was playing on the radio when Karis opened the passenger door of our Caravan and climbed inside. My thought patterns automatically caused me to hold my hand high, fingers up, palm out toward her. She responded with a resounding high-five slap.

Driving home I realized that a time is coming when Karis will be the one waiting behind the high school in her SUV for her son or daughter to get done with athletic practice. When that happens, I won't be part of her daily life like I am now. But even in those twilight years God will still have many high-five moments for me to enjoy. I hope that when that time comes for you and me, we will be found faithfully filling the position that God has assigned us on His playing field.

And when the evening shades of our lives finally wash the dark shadows of death over us, we can look forward to walking through the front doors of heaven and finding a Friend holding up two nail-scarred hands to slap us a double high five and welcome us home.

19

LASAGNA WARS

I initially realized the confidence my wife, Darcy, placed in my child-care abilities the first morning after I put her on the plane to visit her mother. She's normally up and in position by 6 a.m. fixing the kids' lunches. So there I was, up and in position to make their lunches. But when Colt walked into the kitchen, the confused look on his face told me I was doing something wrong.

"What are you doing, Dad?"

"I'm going to make everyone's lunch for school."

"Why? Mom's already packed all the lunches for the entire week." He went on to show me the drill. "First, you go to the freezer here. All of our sandwiches are made and have our name on the cellophane . . . one for each day she's gone. Then you go over to the counter here [there were three baskets with assorted options] and you pick a fruit, throw in a snack, and grab a juice box." He put everything into a lunch bag and folded the top down.

"But it's frozen," I said, trying to figure out some flaw in the system that might justify a need for my services.

"It's thawed by lunchtime, Dad. It's perfect."

And so it was. An efficient system left in place by a woman who knew full well that if the kids' nutritional needs were left completely to my devices, she'd come home to offspring who would make great poster children for crop failure.

I struggle at certain things, and cooking is one of them. I have made two cakes in my life, both of them for Darcy's birthday. One was on her seventeenth. I was trying to impress her with how deep my love for her really flowed. The second was for her twenty-second birthday. On both occasions, I realized after the fact that in the time it took me to make those cakes, I could have gotten part-time jobs and made enough money to buy a gigantic

Safeway cake from some canceled wedding or bar mitzvah. I used to make pretty good ice, but since we bought the refrigerator that makes it for you, I've lost my touch.

It's not hard for me to admit that I'm average in most things that I do. Average people who work hard usually get above-average results. It's tough, however, when you're actually way below average, and all the sweat you can muster doesn't seem to increase your chances. I never learned my way around a kitchen, and in my attempts to come up to speed in the culinary bracket, I've fallen farther behind.

One day Darcy and I were having one of those "married with children" talks about who's going to die first. When we considered the possibility that she might be the one, I immediately assured her I wouldn't be far behind. She thought about it a moment and then asked, "Starvation?" I simply nodded.

There's a lot of room in the family of God for people with below-average talents. The Gerasene demoniac comes to mind (Mark 5:1–20; Luke 8:26–39). He was naked, crazy, dangerous, and unredeemed. After he was transformed through a heart encounter with the Savior, he really stepped up his game. Jesus obviously saw his potential. In fact, when he asked if he could accompany Jesus and the disciples back across the lake in their boat, Jesus instead encouraged him to go and tell his family all of the great things that had happened. The next time Jesus and his disciples were in his region (known as the Decapolis), they were on foot. And everywhere they went, they found people who already believed in Jesus. Apparently the friend they made in the tombs at Gerasene ended up telling a lot more than his family about God's mighty work.

As you can see, below-average people can do extraordinary things. There's no need to despair because you can't be the ocean liner you'd hoped to be. The little dinghies with the oars are the boats that usually save people.

Since there's lots of room in God's family for below-average people, we need to make sure that our families reflect the same heart attitude. Where people come up short, we need to show grace. When people try hard and fail, we need to offer patience.

I was thinking of that when it came time to fix dinner for the crew. In Darcy's absence, she had left a menu and instructions hanging by a magnet on the door of the refrigerator. "Dinner: get the Stouffer's lasagna in freezer and follow the microwave instructions." I guess I should have read more carefully. I went to the freezer and grabbed the microwaveable lasagna sitting on the top shelf. I didn't notice at the time that it happened to be made by some company called Claim Jumpers rather than Stouffer's.

Because our big microwave oven was being repaired, we were temporarily using a smaller one. After I got the Claim Jumpers lasagna out of its box, I realized that it was long and narrow and wouldn't fit into the microwave (though the Stouffer's would have fit perfectly). No problem. I would just cut it in half. Easier said than done. It was frozen brick-hard, and the big knife I hacked it with didn't faze it.

Men love tools of mass destruction, and this was one of those situations that called for one. I took the lasagna to my workbench in the garage, got out my miter box and saw, and started slicing it in half. But the cheese really gummed up the saw. I could only make it about halfway through when everything got slow going. No problem;

I just needed to bring on the heavy artillery—my cordless Mikita power saw. I ripped right through that frozen lasagna as if it was soft butter. I was doing all of this just after dark with the garage door up and myself backlit by the workbench lights to anyone passing by at street level.

Meanwhile, a college student, who was in the neighborhood selling magazine subscriptions, happened to see me in the garage working at my bench. When the whine of the saw stopped, I heard him calling to me from the darkness out in the driveway. I walked from my workbench to the garage door to see what he wanted.

"What's up?" I asked him. Before he introduced himself, he looked over my shoulder and asked, "Did I just see you sawing a lasagna in half?"

"Yeah, I'm fixing dinner." Apparently, that was all he needed to know before he decided to skip his magazine spiel and move on to my neighbor's house, wanting nothing more to do with the power-saw-wielding nut job at mine.

20

EXTRAORDINARILY
AVERAGE

Comparison is the poison pill of parenting. It not only kills your joy, but it snuffs out your ability to mine the ore of potentiality that has been placed deep down inside your "average" child—a child who happens to be made in God's image. And what makes it all worse is the painful reality that any time we let ourselves compare our children to the airbrushed ideals that our culture celebrates, our children realize it. They get that gut-level feeling deep down inside that they have fallen short of our hopes for them.

It's easy to trip into this trap. We live in the secular

context of a 24/7 worship service that sings praises to the beauty, talent, and accomplishments of youth. And often, it's a good friend, grandparent, or older sibling who leads the cultural praise choir. Batting averages, GPAs, Photoshopped looks, class rank, dress sizes, and major awards become the unconscious grading scale. And even though only a precious few hit those standards, they nevertheless become the benchmark for too many disappointed parents.

The problem even laps over into Christians, causing a sort of spiritual class envy. You observe what appears to be a teenage apostle-in-the-making who can't wait to get to church, reads his Bible every day, engages the adults around him in intelligent conversation, and never falls short of making his parents look good. And then you study your son, a boy . . .

. . . who seldom goes to church without a fight,

. . . who is fortunate to remember his shoes, let alone his Bible,

. . . whose head may be on frontward but whose hat rarely is,

. . . and who can't seem to put together a two-syllable response to a Sunday Bible class teacher's question.

It's like a bad episode of *American Idol* with a judge cleaning his teeth on the bones left after his critique of your child's performance.

But really, this is not about your children. I just used them as a convenient introduction to the idea of comparison. This is about all of us. We are all compulsive comparers. But it's time for us to put the brakes on that compulsion.

Stop for a second. Step back. Take in the big picture. Who's the mastermind behind the comparison compulsion of the world anyway? Last time I checked, it was that liar who slithered into Eden. I haven't heard that he's changed his tune. His lies about what's important are still lies, even if the rank and file of an entire generation embraces them with all they've got.

Then there is this other voice out there that whispers your name. And even though the culture may try to drown Him out, His voice still slips through the clamor of comparison: "Come unto Me. I will never leave you. I am the way. I will give you rest. Be anxious for nothing.

Cast all your cares upon Me. I'll be with you always. If you have Me, you have life." That is the Voice that longs to echo in our hearts when we despair of being average. He wants us to see with His eyes and realize just how extraordinary average can really be.

Take the stories of four average people in the Bible. These unremarkable people put what little they had at the disposal of the Savior, but the impact of their contributions exceeded those of any member of who's who in youth culture today.

There was the teenage girl who was asked by God to offer up her womb. He just needed it for nine months. It almost cost her a fiancé. It surely cost her good reputation. But the world was in desperate need of a Savior, so this teenage girl with no social pedigree said yes and, in the process, became one of the most revered women in history.

There was a boy with a meager lunch who handed it over to a man who had the recipe for the bread of life. His average offering was turned into a feast that guaranteed that none of the five thousand people around him went home hungry.

There was that hardscrabble young disciple who reluctantly placed his filthy foot into the hands of the Son of Man and discovered the secret to a thorough bath for his soul. He learned what God can do when we hand over the vilest parts of our lives to His cleansing grace.

Then there was the ordinary businessman who offered his own burial tomb—a man-made cave in the side of a hill—to a crucified Redeemer. That hole in the rock became the staging area for His transformation into the resurrection and the life. He can do the same with you in spite of how "ordinary" your life seems to you.

Ordinary people? There's really no such thing. Each of us is created in the image of the God of the universe. Each of us carries the capacity to one day have all our ordinariness peeled away like a threadbare thrift store shirt, revealing the glorious perfection of what God intended us to be all along. In His eyes, there are no ordinary people. How can we be when we were created by an extraordinary God? A God who offers to give you Himself so you can find in Him the kind of life you want to live.

I love this quote from James R. Sizoo: "Let it never be forgotten that glamour is not greatness; applause is not fame; prominence is not eminence. The man of the hour is not apt to be the man of the ages. A stone may sparkle, but that does not make it a diamond; people may have money, but that does not make them a success. It is what faithful people do that really counts and determines the course of history."[1]

Extraordinarily average? It may not be the life you dreamed of. It may not have the glamour, high achievement, headline-making success or widespread influence you had planned for. But if God is the architect of your Plan B life, it's actually . . . better.

Why compare, when you already have it all?

NOTES

Chapter 6: For Our Tomorrows They Gave Their Todays
1. James Bradley with Ron Powers, *Flags of Our Fathers* (New York: Bantam Books, 2000).
2. Ibid., 247.

Chapter 7: Sticking to Your Post
1. From the *Plebe's Handbook* (Reef Points: United States Naval Academy).

Chapter 20: Extraordinarily Average
1. James R. Sizoo, "Glamour Is Not Greatness," *Bits and Pieces*, 22 June 1995, 11. Available at http://net.bible.org/illustration.php?id=2370. Accessed 9 June 2010.

Dr. Tim and Darcy Kimmel

Dr. Tim Kimmel and his wife, Darcy, are the founders of Family Matters. Tim speaks throughout the U.S. and Canada on how to create family relationships that not only bring the best out in each other but lead each family member to live a life that makes an eternal difference.

He has more than 800,000 books and videos in print, including the Gold Medallion winner *Grace Based Parenting*, *Why Christian Kids Rebel*, and *Little House on the Freeway*. Tim is a frequent guest on national radio and television shows. He enjoys life with his wife, their four adult children, their children's spouses, and his growing number of grandchildren.

building grace-based relationships

Family Matters educates, encourages and equips families to:

- live relevant, joyful and victorious lives

- bring the best out of each other in their daily relationships.

- pass a legacy of God's grace from one generation to the next.

In a sentence, the grace-based strategy is simply treating the members of your family the way God treats the members of His family.

To learn more about building grace-based relationships,
go to www.familymatters.net

blog · audios and videos · quarterly download of "Heart of the Home" ·
facebook · twitter · resources · speaking and conference schedule · articles

13402 N. Scottsdale Road, Suite A-120
Scottsdale, AZ 85254

Share Your Thoughts

With the Author: Your comments will be forwarded to the author when you send them to *zauthor@zondervan.com*.

With Zondervan: Submit your review of this book by writing to *zreview@zondervan.com*.

Free Online Resources at
www.zondervan.com

Zondervan AuthorTracker: Be notified whenever your favorite authors publish new books, go on tour, or post an update about what's happening in their lives at www.zondervan.com/authortracker.

Daily Bible Verses and Devotions: Enrich your life with daily Bible verses or devotions that help you start every morning focused on God. Visit www.zondervan.com/newsletters.

Free Email Publications: Sign up for newsletters on Christian living, academic resources, church ministry, fiction, children's resources, and more. Visit www.zondervan.com/newsletters.

Zondervan Bible Search: Find and compare Bible passages in a variety of translations at www.zondervanbiblesearch.com.

Other Benefits: Register yourself to receive online benefits like coupons and special offers, or to participate in research.

ZONDERVAN®

ZONDERVAN.com/
AUTHORTRACKER
follow your favorite authors